RESTORING AMERICA

RESTORING AMERICA

BY RETURNING TO ITS CONSTITUTION

HOWELL WOLTZ

The International Centre for Justice

International Centre for Justice
Bukowinska 2, m. 194
02-703, Warsaw
Poland

Other books by Howell Woltz
Justice Denied: the United States v. the People (2010, 2014, 2016)
The Way Back to America: 10 steps to restore the United States to constitutional government (2014)
The Path: A Spiritual Guide for the Fifth Age (2015)
Justice Restored: 10 steps to end mass incarceration in America (2016)
Gulag Ameryka (2018- Europe)

Published by The International Centre for Justice, Warsaw, Poland
June of 2018

ISBN 978-1-7195-7863-9

Back cover photo by David Rosen

Typesetting services by BOOKOW.COM

DEDICATION

This book is dedicated to those who fought so bravely to create and protect our nation, not only with sword and gun, but pen. Equal to their courage is that of those who remained at home and stood by them in their fight, rather than asking those brave souls to accept the temporary security of tyranny over liberty.

We face a danger equal to that of our First Revolution in 1776 today, but against a force more insidious as they have not the courage to fight openly, but only through deceit. These enemies, use stealth from inside our nation's capital to destroy our Constitution. Each of these so-called "Progressives" of both political parties took an oath of office to uphold it, but they only undermine it.

Now that the power of their shadow government is nearly complete, they are openly conspiring to undo a presidential election and reduce us to the goal of Progressivism—a modern version of feudalism with us as the servants and these unelected Elites as Masters. There is nothing new about that. Such ideas are regressive and as old as slavery itself.

I speak of the elected and unelected deep State Progressives who now control our government from within and have sworn to remove our Constitution and its protections.

But we don't need a Revolution. We just need to take our lives back from the Progressives now running our country by forcing them to live by our contract.

That, by the way, is the United States Constitution, and "they" stand in breach of it.

No, we don't need another Revolution—well not just yet—but we must force them by any means necessary to start living within the clear mandates of their authority, or we will.

It is time we woke them up—all of them—the disdainful Democrats who call us 'deplorable' for loving our country and way of life, as well as the equally disgusting Republicans who promise 'less government' and 'less spending' every two years to get elected and immediately prove themselves to be despicable liars at every opportunity they have to expand their power, enrich themselves, or spend our money. They all need a timeout.

So when I saw someone come into power that so rattled these deep state operatives and liars of both sides to make them pull out all the stops to destroy him—I knew that he must be the one we've been praying for, so I started putting ink to paper with a plan to take us back to Rule of Law. Back to limited federal government. Back to our Constitution.

Welcome to the Devolution.

Acknowledgments

I would like to thank the International Centre for Justice in Warsaw, Poland for making this book possible—but I must also thank U.S. President Donald J. Trump for giving our nation its first opportunity in decades to actually realize much-needed change. If he were not in The White House, I would never have wasted my time writing this book.

President Trump has correctly identified the problems—the Progressive grip on our nation, the lack of truth or accountability in the few remaining media outlets, the incredible concentration of federal power in unelected hands, and the corruption that embodies America's two-party (one-minded) political system. In other words, we actually may have a chance to see these things corrected by this man whom so many—on both sides—love to hate.

The status quo of the past three decades marches our nation's chosen way of life to a slow and agonizing death. A Disruptor is our only chance.

So "Long live the Disruptor,"

And....I believe we finally have a Commander-in-Chief for our Devolution.

Back to Constitution and Government by and for, the People.

Howell Woltz

May 24, 2018

CONTENTS

Foreword

THE United States of America is not just a nation forged from 50 separate and independent nation-states, it is an idea. Our Founders believed that mankind was capable of self government in a state of complete freedom by joining sovereign, human-scale and relatively homogenous units of government together into a confederation, for the purposes of common defense, trade, and currency.

That was a fairly new idea back in 1776—in fact, it was radical—but the American experiment in freedom is nearing its end.

That is, if we let these unelected Elites known as "Progressives," have their way. Have you ever taken the time to learn what the founders of this movement proposed? It will shock you, both at why they think of themselves as Elites (better than those they govern), and how close they have come to achieving most if not all of their goals.

Just for a moment, imagine the stark fear that rattled the dictatorial world of elitist regimes—such as Europe's kings and despots—when they heard that 13 small colonies an ocean away had chosen self-government. Think of the trepidation felt in their hearts seven years later when they learned this rag-tag army of citizen-soldiers defending their freedom with their own weapons had defeated the world's greatest army of conscripts and mercenaries ever assembled.

This idea of freedom and self-government was certainly not European. The European settlers did not bring this idea to the shores of North

America, they found it here. It is totally American, and I for one want no other type of government to ever reach these shores.

"For his ideas about the emergence of governing institutions out of the state of Nature, Locke looked to Native America."[1] It wasn't John Locke who taught America about freedom and liberty, it was America that taught John Locke.

The first known European expedition to our shores was led by Hernando de Soto in 1539.[2] He and his men—and their herd of swine—unwittingly sentenced the native people to death by spreading smallpox, which killed an estimated 92% of my Native American ancestors. When my Welsh ancestors arrived roughly 85 years later in 1613, the continent was empty by comparison. When my Jewish ancestors arrived from Switzerland in 1738, it was again populated and the Native American idea of complete freedom by natural law without any leader other than one chosen had overcome the minds of the European colonists as thoroughly as their smallpox had overcome the natives.

And American Elites are in a similar state of shock and fear today at the Trump Revolution of 2016 just as their predecessors of old Europe were in 1776 of the first.

Just watch and listen to the media and the Progressives who people it. Listen to their dire warnings of apocalypse from their billionaire backers who are spending fortunes now to remove our duly-elected president and trying to take our constitutional rights "to protect us." Protect us from whom and what? It is their ideas and programs of the past century that are the greatest danger to us and our way of life. It isn't our guns or free speech that will be our undoing. It is their absence and being forced into Orwellian sameness of mind and speech that will destroy us—which has always been the Progressive's admitted endgame since the 1890s.

---

[1] Editorial: "John Locke and the Example of Native America" by Leonard P. Liggio, Dec. 1, 1979, Also see https://www.youtube.com/watch?v=DgZcsZqY20Y

[2] De Soto found a Spaniard, Juan Ortiz, living among the Mocoso people, who had been captured by the Uzita while searching for the lost Narváez expedition, but de Soto's was the first recorded expedition. https://en.wikipedia.org/wiki/Hernando_de_Soto

Progressivism is What we Must Fear the Most

Orwell's book, *1984,* was not just a story. It was the gameplan of British Progressives from the orbit of Oxford University Professor John Ruskin and his student, Sir Cecil Rhodes as well as their more intellectually inclined brothers of The Fabians, whose members included the mastermind of debasing the money of Western nations—John Maynard Keynes —as well as intellectuals of the day, George Bernard Shaw and Sidney Webb, among others.[3] George Orwell was briefly one of them, then disgusted by what he learned of their true mission, he wrote what appeared to be a novel—perhaps out of fear of reprisal—but it was his imagined result of the Rhodesian plan of world domination by a small group of Elites—and that, by the way, still is their plan.

These wealthy men from England's upper-crust openly espoused ruling the world—benevolently, of course—but ruling it nonetheless, because they believed and stated clearly that we "the hairy unwashed" (since updated to "deplorables") are incapable of governing ourselves.

America's Progressive tyrants are just as unaccustomed to loss today, as their European predecessors were the last time we whipped them in the 1780s. You can see it and hear it on almost every mainstream media outlet today. They simply will not accept that *We the People* actually beat them. Mrs. Clinton, the loser, still appears to be campaigning, in hopes that her Deep State cohorts will yet save her. The truly scary part is that they just might. They have proven themselves to be completely lawless, in fact, we see today that they believe themselves to be above our laws— they are 'the Elites.' Perhaps now you better understand their arrogance. It is their belief system.

They honestly believe this, as you will read from those who founded their movement.

---

[3]Griffin, Edward. The Creature From Jekyll Island: A Second Look at the Federal Reserve, p. 87-88. 106, 109-111, 239, 273, 483

It is clear today. Rather than graciously accepting defeat as Richard Nixon did to John Kennedy when he won the popular vote (but lost the electoral vote), President Trump's Progressive opponent put herself and the Soros-backed movement on an unparalleled attempt to overthrow the winner. Such amazing gall....

For the record, I am not a Republican proxy. In my opinion, President John F. Kennedy was the last truly conservative president we had other than perhaps Ronald Reagan in some aspects, so I was pleased when free-trader Nixon—the man who would open our borders and pocketbooks to the world, remove the last backing to our currency, and sell us out to Progressive notions—lost the election. To Nixon's credit, however, he did not question Kennedy's win or try to bring him down through subterfuge. Even Nixon knew why we have an Electoral College and bowed out gracefully.

And to make a point, we have that unique aspect of electing a president because 'The United States of America,' is plural and was stated as such for much of our history. "The United States *are* (at war, disappointed in, upset by, etc.) with _______." That is because the Founders intended each nation-state to be a separate laboratory of freedom on how best to improve the lives of citizens while living within the intentionally loose agreement formed between their people and the federal government.

So as stated in the opening paragraph, *We the People* agreed to join in a federal entity for just three purposes—1) mutual defense against external enemies, 2) a common currency, and 3) open trade between our respective nation-States.

That was and is our design, and that is why we have an Electoral College. Each nation-state votes for the candidate their people chose, which is a very important component. We are not a 'democracy' as you hear Progressives scream at every venue, we are a constitutional republic comprised of 50 sovereign states. I challenge anyone to show me the word *democracy* in the United States Constitution. We are a republic—with some democratic components, of course—but with strict limitations on what rights we can vote away from ourselves, which is the only reason we still have some left.

And the reason our Founders established the Electoral College system —and the reason the Progressives are now trying to tear it down—was put on stark display in 2016. *"The Associated Press"* the headlines roared, *"finds that Clinton won 487 counties nationwide, compared with 2,626 for President-elect Donald Trump."*[4] A landslide for President Trump, right?

Well, according the them, no. And this report did not come from FOX News, as you might expect, but from mainstream sources to dispute conservative claims that *only 57 counties nationwide voted for their hero, Hillary Clinton.* It was 487, nationwide!, they proudly proclaimed, while refusing to delve into her amazing loss in the other 2,626 counties where the bulk of Americans live, die, and exist, outside the awareness (or concern) of coastal elites and Progressives. A map of the United States showing the county-by-county vote is red with a few blue freckles, rimmed in coastal elite blue. I hope you will go to the link below and see it for yourself. You will then understand their fear.[5] They will never rule this nation of 'deplorables' as Mrs. Clinton describes us, without getting rid of the Electoral College, when it is clear that she and the Progressives have no concern for us or our well-being. This is an almost solid red nation.

Progressives are calling for the end of the Electoral College so they can expunge this last acknowledgement of our true form of government. If they succeed, they will have won. Elite 'Progressives' in New York, San Francisco, Chicago, and Los Angeles will then rule us all—their stated goal back in 1913—but one look at the map in the footnote below also tells the real story as to why they must be stopped. Almost no one in

---

[4]http://www.dispatch.com/content/stories/national_world/2016/12/06/1206-clinton-won-487-counties.html

[5]http://i0.wp.com/metrocosm.com/wp-content/uploads/2016/11/election-2016-county-map.png?resize=600\%2C386

America between those blue coasts wants them. The map makes this absolutely clear.

And no one since President JFK has really tried to stop the Progressives, which is why he was killed in the opinion of many, and we see they will stop at nothing today— legal or illegal —to stop Donald J. Trump. They know he may be the next to sincerely attempt to put an end to those who swore to destroy our individual liberties—the Progressives.

Having been very much alive through Kennedy's time in office as well as Donald J. Trump's (almost as lengthy) tenure, I see them as soulmates.

1. Both were/are very conservative economically, as example, calling for major tax cuts, severe reductions in regulations, and an overall downsizing of federal government.

2. Both were/are scamps when it comes to women. Kennedy brought them into the White House for sex on a regular basis (including actress, Marilyn Monroe) and Trump, as head of the Miss America Pageant, appears to have been equally active in private practice.

3. But both of them also attracted amazing women to marry. Melania Trump is the most graceful first lady perhaps in history, but for sure, John Kennedy's wife, Jacqueline, was a close second.

4. Both hated Progressivism and fought it.

5. Both understood that printing fake money against debt would eventually consume all the nation's resources, and cutting it off was the only way to kill Progressivism. Kennedy suggested an end to the Federal Reserve (and ordered the printing of U.S. Treasury Notes weeks before his murder), while Trump is also open to a return to real money.

6. Both promote/promoted a strong America—not to fight wars, but to prevent them.

The fact that so-called Progressive 'anti-constitutionalists' have entrenched themselves at the very highest levels of government would be as offensive to John Kennedy as it is to Donald Trump and I believe they both understood that Progressives have come very close to achieving their goal this past century, as the statistics show.

A handful of Progressive corporations now control 90% of the world's assets, resources and information. I contend this was not an accident. Why? Because I've read Sir Cecil Rhodes plan for doing just that and the history of how he, for all intents and purposes, appears to have achieved it, as you will within. They also planned to control the media to keep us 'hairy unwashed' deplorables in line. So how did that work our for the Progressives?

Pretty darn well. In 1983, there were 50 media corporations.[6] Today, just five mostly Progressive monopolies control over 80% of world news, as we will discuss in Chapter Two.[7] A handful of Progressive-owned banks control all of the western world's currency exchange and have the power to manipulate the price of real commodities, while our food supply is virtually controlled by four international agroopolies. Bayer/Monsanto, Dupont/Dow, ChemChina/Sygenta, and BASF control 60% of the seed and fertiliser markets worldwide.

Such concentration of power and wealth was the stated goal of Progressives a century ago and in almost every aspect of our lives, they have achieved it.

In spite of our glorious beginnings whipping the Elites, our nation has once again fallen under their despotic rule. Not by force of arms or invasion —these people are too cowardly for that—but rather by the corrosive and arrogant policies carrying the misnomer of "Progressivism." This idcology was forced on *We the People* by the likes of Presidents Theodore

---

[6]The New Media Monopoly, by Ben H. Bagdikian, Beacon Press, Boston (2004), p. 16
[7]Ibid. p. 3

Roosevelt (after his term as President, he became a vocal proponent to try to get the support of the extraordinarily wealthy backers of the Progressive movement), Thomas Woodrow Wilson, Franklin Delano Roosevelt, George H.W. Bush, William Jefferson Clinton, George W. Bush, and more recently, Barack Hussein Obama—all believing that an unelected class of professional bureaucrats (under their control, of course) were better qualified to govern our lives than we—or even our elected officials—are capable of doing for ourselves.

This form of society is not new and certainly not *progressive*, as it harkens back to feudal days when (other) lords ruled and peasants labored. It is *regressive*.

It took mankind millenia to throw off the yoke of similar despots, before *progressing* to the idea that man can be free in thought, speech, and life without bounds or limit—as long as he does no harm to his or her neighbor—who is endowed with those same rights.

Natural law, as defined as far back as Aristotle in 350 B.C. in his *Nicomachean Ethics* was the moral compass our Founding Fathers believed should govern, and these same *radicals* who founded our nation believed that these rights and freedoms were not only "self-evident" but of divine origin. The founders of the Progressive Movement believed (and still do believe) that they are of divine origin—as gods on earth—destined to rule us. You will read their own words from then and now. I'm not making this up.....they believe that.

But our Founders made a huge mistake. By restricting these "self-evident" rights of divine origin only to white men, the Founders made the grievous error of intellectual hypocrisy that later gave Progressivism the opening to try to destroy what they created. If these rights were truly of divine origin and so "self-evident," why were Native Americans, women, and African-Americans excluded from the process?

This horrible mistake has allowed Progressives to challenge the very core of our nation's beliefs, putting most of our freedoms at risk while cementing their power over us under the guise of *protecting* us from ourselves.

Limited government became unlimited as burgeoning bureaucracies usurped powers granted solely to our elected representatives in Congress and the Executive Branch and took over the Judiciary—the branch of government we were to control—as well. Progressives not only began writing their own laws to control our every movement and thought, they have now usurped the authority to enforce and punish them.

There are in fact so many of these federal agencies intentionally created under the Progressive Movement making up their own laws (and enforcing them) that Hudson Hollister, counsel for the House Oversight Committee, recently stated that he could not get an answer from the Office of Management and Budget or Government Accounting Office as to the actual number of federal and quasi-federal agencies Congress is now funding. They have simply lost count.[8]

Congress abdicated most of its constitutional law-making authority to these unelected agencies and bureaucrats under the rule of so-called Progressive leaders of the 20th and 21st century, and they can no longer even tell us how many of them there are. Progressive bureaucrats have used their unaccountable power to disenfranchise citizens who fail to embrace their ideology, while protecting those who do.

If that sounds outrageous, one only needs to look at Progressive Lois Lerner's unrelenting and unlawful attacks on conservative groups while heading the IRS charitable organizations division (and later, the IRS itself) after refusing to cooperate in a federal probe that revealed The Clinton Foundation garnered tens of millions in foreign 'donations' without declaring them between 2001 and 2003 in its 'pay to play' scheme.

---

[8]http://dailycaller.com/2013/05/03/the-government-has-no-idea-how-many-agencies-it-has/2/

James Comey, the man now trashing President Trump on a book tour, took over that investigation in 2002 to see that it did not lead to criminal indictments of his Progressive mentors, Bill and Hillary Clinton.

Rod Rosenstein—Deputy Director of the FBI who brought in Robert Mueller in 2017 to attack President Trump, oversaw that Tax Division investigation of The Clinton Foundation for the Department of Justice from 2001 to 2005 and he and Robert Mueller—the former FBI chief now in charge of the witch hunt intended to depose Trump—quietly dismissed the case against his Progressive allies—the Clintons—after James Comey swept the grand jury findings under the rug and refused to prosecute. I'm sure any American will recognize all of these names, as they are still protecting the criminals of Progressivism while pursuing those in favor of our constitutional form of government—and trying to destroy the man we elected to stop them.

They have proven their willingness to protect their own by any means—legal or illegal—while trashing their enemies. Comey, Lerner, Mueller, and Rosenstein were never intended to enforce the law, they were put in those positions of power to choose who suffered its overreach, and who was protected, as their actions have now proven in spades.

But let's delve a little deeper. This unknown number of federal agencies have invented so many laws for the Comeys, Muellers and Rosensteins to choose from, that the average American now commits three 'felonies' a day—and does not even know it. These unauthorised 'federal' crimes are so obscure and punishment for them so unnatural that few would consider the behavior to be morally wrong.[9]

Have you mistreated a mailbag? Have you released a mammal from a net? Have you collected rainwater off your own roof? How about this— Have you ever *thought* about committing a crime? If you answered 'yes'

---

[9] *Three Felonies a Day: How the Feds Target the Innocent,* by Attorney Harvey A. Silverglate, with Foreword by Harvard Law Professor, Alan M. Dershowitz, (2009) Encounter Books, New York and London.

to any of these—and you are black, brown, or conservative—watch out. You might be next.

Under the Constitution, criminal laws are the province of the States to determine and punish with only three exceptions: 1) Piracy on the High Seas, 2) Counterfeiting of currency and government securities, and 3) Treason. The Tenth Amendment forbade the adding of other such authorities or duties not stated, reserving them for the States and people, including their punishment.

'Progressives' of both parties have exceeded this mandate by fabricating a total of 314,000 statutes outlawing what throughout most of history were considered normal human behaviors. That is not a misprint, by the way. Three hundred fourteen thousands ways have been invented to put you in prison.

"Why?," any sane person might ask, "would they do such a thing?" The only answer I can come up with is so that Progressives such as the ones named above can control (and remove) dissidents at will and imprison them, any time, for any (or no) reason—even from the White House—while protecting their own from force of the same laws.

It's Mafia.02. And Mueller, Lerner, Rosenstein, Comey—as well as Andrew Weissman, Andrew McCabe, Peter Strzok, Lisa Page, Bruce Ohr, James Clapper, John Brennan—the top tier of government and intelligence—*are the gangsters*. If all I have uncovered is true, the set-up for Mrs. Clinton to win the election by those listed in this paragraph, and their subsequent efforts to depose a duly elected president who beat her, would punish them each for life in prison—or worse—using the same laws they have used to target and imprison groups that 1) are not part of their Elitist Progressive Movement or 2) might try to stop them.

At some point, when there are more things you can't do than you can do, you can't keep on claiming to be free.

And one look at the breakdown of who these real gangsters have thrown in their prisons gives the true picture of the Elitists' mentality and goals. The laws they created (until the advent of Trump) targeted mostly poor black people, poor brown people, and white conservatives. That more or less describes the prison population of the United States—now the largest in world history. I've filed motions in or worked on over 400 federal criminal cases since 2006 and most of those men were black, closely followed by brown, and the rest, were white conservatives with only one exception—world famous ultra runner Charlie Engle. He's a great guy, but liberal.

So if Progressive Elitists did not intend this outcome, why are most of the 71 million Americans[10] who have suffered this ruin—approximately one in every four adults—black, brown or white conservatives? These people were destroyed with laws specifically designed to remove them from the voting pool, seems to be the only possible answer to that question. They wanted young black males out of the way, so they created laws that gave penalties for watered-down cocaine (known as crack, used almost exclusively by blacks), at 100 times the sentences given to Elite country-clubbers who sniff the pure uncut stuff up their noses.

There is no way anyone could write such a stupid law unless it was intended to remove young blacks from the streets—for decades—and disenfranchise them for life.

If that sounds outrageous, you should read the works of John Ruskin, Cecil Rhodes, Herbert Croly, John Dewey, and President Woodrow Wilson—the proponents of the 'Progressive' ideology propagated to end constitutional America—by replacing it with their own kind to rule us all. They were open about their belief that people 'of color' were inferior to them, and that conservative whites were their enemy. It is in their writings. They not only said it, they wrote that they believed they were superior to *We the People* and must rule us to protect us from ourselves.

---

[10] "The U.S. Department of Justice estimates that 71 million Americans—approximately 25%—have a criminal record." BNA Criminal Law Reporter, May 19, 2010, Vol. 87, No. 7, by Eric M. Fish

These targeted laws have caused the disenfranchisement of 71 million Americans just since I was in college. They lost their right to vote or participate in many government programs, though still forced to fund them. This loss of rights, I fear, was the Progressive goal of creating so many illegitimate statutes, but whether by intent or not, they have effectively disenfranchised one quarter of all adult American citizens of their constitutional rights—mostly black, brown or conservative.

Their victims not only can't vote, they can't defend themselves or their families. They can't get good jobs, and most of them are returned to prison by a system also designed by Progressives to keep the "underclass" in that rotating cycle for as many years as possible. And now they are forced to work as prison laborers at less than third-world wages.

These new American plantations house factories for the créme de la créme of big business and multi-nationals such as IBM, Boeing, Motorola, Microsoft, AT&T Wireless, Texas Instrument, Dell, Compaq, Honeywell, Hewlett-Packard, Nortel, Lucent Technologies, 3Com, Intel, Northern Telecom, TWA, Nordstrom's, Revlon, Macy's, Pierre Cardin, [and] Target Stores, just to name a few. They pay wages beneath the hourly rate of Haiti, for skilled American workers. The "minimum" wage is $5.00….per month. The Progressives who founded this system claim it is not "slavery" under the 13th amendment because their slaves are paid something, though often, so were the slaves of old. This modern version of slavery also leaves no choice but to work for the master. If a prisoner refuses, he or she is put in solitary confinement (a.k.a. "Segregated Housing Unit" or SHU) until they come around—very similar to their predecessors.

Admittedly, this idea of enslaving one's own citizens to use as industrial workers is not new. The difference is that we—America—used to fight and hate people who did the same thing, until Progressives in Congress and our courts copied the very methods used by the German Nazis to enslave their Jewish citizens and political dissidents for national industries in the 1940s, as did the Soviet Union and Communist China in the 20th century. They targeted the groups to be enslaved with behavior-specific laws, eliminated due process of law in their judicial systems, and granted immunity to the judges and prosecutors who committed these crimes against their fellow citizens. It works every time.

Progressives in Congress under President Franklin D. Roosevelt moved this overreach of federal powers into high gear by creating a federal *criminal* code (Title 18- Crimes and Criminal Procedure) in 1948 to be used to imprison us lesser beings and 'deplorables'—though prohibited by Constitution and never approved by the U.S. Senate,[11] their successors have since voted to criminalize over 4,000 human behaviors—up from the three allowed them to "punish" under our Constitution.

Congress must also take credit for further violating its Constitutional limits by assigning criminal punishment to more than 10,000 *Civil* Statutes—in another amazing Constitution-defying stunt.

So that's 14,000 "felonies" illegally created by Congress—though only authorized to punish three in our Constitution. How did the other 300,000 laws come into being?

In short—not legally as well—but that is the number of statutes The American Legislative Exchange Council estimates have been added under "Administrative law" which was the system put in place by Progressives to hijack our government. Rather than being passed by Congress or signed into law by a president as required by the Constitution, an unelected bureaucrat wrote them and started having people arrested for their violation. How can they be considered valid if our elected representatives did not ever pass them, and how can American citizens be imprisoned by laws that are themselves illegal?

---

[11] "Title 18 is alleged to have been passed into law on June 25, 1948. However, Congress was not in session for 36 days during that period and could not have passed any legislation into law during the recess that extend prior to and after June 25,1948."
https://www.scribd.com/document38905483Title18hasneverbeenapprovedbyCongress07-30-07

The answer again is—not legally—but American citizens go to prison every day for them, while Congress passes $1.3 trillion budget-busters as they did in March of 2018, to fund the Progressive agencies and gangsters of government imprisoning those they consider 'inferior' or a threat to their plan and they do it every day.

Unelected bureaucrats and Progressives such as those heading the nation's most powerful law enforcement agencies named above, are illegally controlling our country and even the 71 million Americans they have disenfranchised, are forced at the point of a gun to pay for it. Though robbed of their rights and access to many government programs, they still have to pay for them, or they will be sent back to prison (or worse).

If that sounds like an overstatement, try not paying your taxes for a few years and see what the Lerners, Comeys, Rosensteins and Muellers do to you. You are not a Clinton or some other self-appointed Elite. You are a serf and when they come to take your property and you try to defend it, they will kill you—which is why they want your gun now instead of later —and have already taken them from one in four poor or conservative American adults, by making them a 'felon.'

Why don't you hear the media talking about this? The question answers itself. The media is controlled by Progressives, as we will prove and discuss in Chapter One.

Can you now see the incredible dangers of Progressivism? Its cadre of Elitist paper shufflers and unelected goons running our nation's law enforcement took over our country without a single shot being fired or a single American voting for them. They quietly stole our nation from us with the troubling assistance of a century of Progressive presidents and congressional leaders acting in direct violation of their oath of office to uphold the United States Constitution.

Instead of keeping that oath, they violated it, ignored it, side-stepped it and many of them did so with intent. It's time to take our country back and we can do it by simply making our federal government go back to our contract now that we finally have someone in the White House who appears to be on our side.

That contract I'm talking about is the one between *We the People* and the federal government—the Constitution of the United States of America.

The Progressives stole our country from us, and I say it's time we took it back.

Howell W. Woltz
May 25, 2018

Chapter 1

WANT TO TEAR DOWN THE STATUE OF A REAL RACIST?

THE insidious ideology of world domination known as "Progressivism," at least in modern times, finds its roots in 1870s England. The British Empire had already begun to wane and its upper class was rapidly losing ground, but socialist Elite, John Ruskin, took it upon himself to teach a course at Oxford University that, unknowingly, and perhaps even unintentionally, would change the course of modern history.

Ruskin said in his lecture, *"My continual aim has been to show the eternal superiority of some men to other, sometimes even of one man to all others."*[1]

In Carroll Quigley's book, *The Anglo-American Estalishment: From Rhodes to Cliveden* (New York: Books in Focus, 1981, pp. ix, 36) he credits Ruskin's speech to a group of Oxford elites drawn from the privileged ruling class of England, for starting the so-called "Progressive" movement that holds the greatest concentration of wealth and power in the world today. The group included some young men, no doubt, from families who were already a bit worn-at-the-knee—and young Cecil Rhodes was among them.

---

[1]See Kenneth Clark, *Ruskin Today* (New York: Holt, Reignhard & Winston, 1964), p. 267.

Young Rhodes was so impressed with Professor Ruskin's speech that he wrote it out in longhand and carried it in his pocket for the next forty years as he became one of the richest men in world history—and, one of its most powerful.[2]

Rhodes went on to create a virtual monopoly over the gold and diamond trade of South Africa, which funded the creation of his secret society to advance the ruling-class-by-Elites ideology of his Oxford professor, John Ruskin.

"Mr. Rhodes was more than the founder of a dynasty." Lord Esher—a member of Rhodes group once wrote, *"He aspired to be the creator of one of those vast semi-religious, quasi-political associations which, like the Society of Jesus, have played so large a part in the history of the world. To be more strictly accurate, he wished to found an Order as the instrument of the will of the Dynasty."*[3]

Rhodes created a "Circle of Initiates" whose executive committee included Lord Brett Stead Esher (quoted above), Lord Alfred Milner (Rhodes' successor running the Progressive cabal), Lord Arthur Balfour, Sir Harry Johnston, Lord Rothschild (Bank of England), and Lord Albert Grey among others—some of the most powerful men in the world—and his committee "continues to exist to this day."[4]

Under the sheep's wool outer appearance of Progressivism that embraces all races, creeds, colors, religions, and encourages open-borders "to all" and every 'ism' known to man—there is a wolf. The wolf will *use* any creed or color as a vehicle to his ultimate power, as long as that subordinate can be controlled by the snobbish Elites who consider them inferior ('deplorable') in every way.

---

[2]Griffin, G. Edward; *The Creature from Jekyll Island: a Second Look at the Federal Reserve;* American Media, Fifth Edition, 2010, fortieth edition, 2016, p. 271.

[3] Carroll Quigley, *The Anglo-American Establishment: From Rhodes to Cliveden* (New York: Books in Focus, 1981) pp. *ix,* 36.

[4]Ibid.

The famous Rhodes Scholarship was established by the terms of Cecil Rhodes' will, and has been used ever since to educate and indoctrinate initiates of the cabal to be put in power in various governments around the world and controlled by it. William Jefferson Clinton, as example, was plucked out of a trailer park community in the backwaters of the poor state of Arkansas by the Rhodes Committee, and you know the rest. He is but one of many—all around the world.

J.P. Morgan was an early adherent to the world-rule-by-Elites philosophy and through his association with Lord Rothschild in London (with whom he stayed when visiting England) lured Princeton University president, Thomas Woodrow Wilson, into the Progressive Movement of world domination already into its third decade of existence. Ultimately, Morgan and his associates financed a three-way race for president—backing them all to insure their loyalty to the cabal—then choosing Wilson at the end as the most pliable and putting him over the finish line to do their bidding.

Taking no chances, J.P. Morgan planted his most trusted man in the White House to see that Wilson did not stray. Colonel Edward Mandell House literally lived with the President during those years and monitored —or more accurately informed—his every move.

As President, this *de facto* founder of the Progressive Movement in America, Woodrow Wilson, was himself a snobbish racist, who personally undid most advances black Americans had made between the Civil War and his being put in office by the Elite bankers of what was then known as "The Money Trust"—headed by J.P. Morgan. As President, Wilson re-instituted segregation throughout government, and the gains made by blacks over half a century evaporated under Progressive Elitism. Blacks, Wilson firmly believed, were inferior to his own race and class.

If Progressive-backed domestic terror groups of today such as 'Antifa' and Black Lives Matter want to tear down the statue of a real racist, I suggest they start with the original founder of their movement in America, Woodrow Wilson.

> *"The Black Justice League, in protests on Princeton University's campus, has drawn wider attention to an inconvenient truth about the university's ultimate star: Woodrow Wilson. The Virginia native was racist, a trait largely overshadowed by his works as Princeton's president, as New Jersey's governor, and, most notably, as the 28th president of the United States.*
>
> *As president, Wilson oversaw unprecedented segregation in federal offices. It's a shameful side to his legacy that came to a head one fall afternoon in 1914 when he threw the civil-rights leader William Monroe Trotter out of the Oval Office."*[5]

Don't send your Progressive hate mail to me. This quote is from an article in *The Atlantic's Politics & Policy Daily* from November of 2015—a Magazine, not known for conservative views—but feel free, Antifa, to tear down President Wilson's statues—all of them—though George Soros and your other backers will never allow you to do it. Woodrow Wilson embodies their own ideology and was one of its founders too—and every one of them feels the same way about you—as you will see soon enough.

What Antifa, Black Lives Matter and other Soros-funded front groups don't seem to realise is that the Elites want them back in chains on the farm—just this time it will be an industrial one in prison.

But Wilson is not only the man who defines the real attitude of Progressivism, he is also the place we need to start to see how this movement has been allowed to undermine our nation and appears to have led to the Second Revolution—the one in 2016, headed by Donald J. Trump instead of George Washington.

---

[5]"The Racist Legacy of Woodrow Wilson.
https://www.theatlantic.com/politics/archive/2015/11/wilson-legacy-racism/417549/

As history has shown, once turned to the dark side, President Woodrow Wilson took to it like a duck to water. Under the heavy hand and guidance of Colonel House, Wilson wrote a book in 1913 advising his intentions to upend the U.S. Constitution. Wilson's book, *The New Freedom,* (as Wilson described putting the yoke back on the less fortunate), said just that. In it, Wilson advocated for the utter dismissal of the document he swore to uphold—the U.S. Constitution.

He wrote, "*We used to say that the idea of government was for every man to be left alone and not interfered with, except when he interfered with somebody else; and that the best government was the government that did as little governing as possible.*" He then went on to declare that he would overturn that basis of our government and pursue the progressive path, which he did with unparalleled zeal and disregard for his oath of office.

In just that one year, 1913, Wilson forced through a constitutionally forbidden private central bank to print money of no real value (The Federal Reserve) which would allow him to fund the build-out of his unelected bureaucratic "Progressive" government under the guidance of his wealthy 'progressive' backers. Wilson also pushed through a constitutionally forbidden 'Capitation tax' (The Sixteenth Amendment)[6] which allowed federal government to reach into the citizens' pockets at will, removing any financial restraints on the growth of federal government or further need to force the States to fund its lawless behavior. If more funding was needed to grow federal government, it could simply be taken from the people through this constitutionally forbidden "Capitation tax."

If that became inconvenient politically, the privately-owned central bank could be asked to print any amount needed—and its owners (Wilson's major 'progressive' handlers, J.P. Morgan, John D. Rockefeller, Paul Warburg, and Lord Rothschild) would profit handsomely from it.

---

[6] Article 1, §9, "Clause 4 of the U.S. Constitution: No Capitation, or other direct, Tax shall be laid, unless in Proportion to the Census or Enumeration herein before directed to be taken."

That is because a federal reserve note has no value. It costs nothing to produce except the paper and ink of which it is made—and its only limitation is that it can only be printed against debt. If that makes no sense, then you understand the process perfectly. You put your nation in debt and print worthless money against it to be used to expand government. Then you borrow more, print more and so on.

The federal reserve note is a *fiat* currency without physical backing of any kind—and its only collateral is debt to other nations or holders of Treasury bills and government debt securities. That's crazy, right? And that is The Federal Reserve foisted on us by the Progressives of our own leadership, but not even part of our government. It was controlled by the richest men in the world—Rockefeller, Morgan, Rothschild, and Warburg.

To force us to use this worthless money, the Progressives ultimately mandated the "Federal Reserve Note" as the currency of the land allowing no other, though the Federal Reserve is neither 'federal' nor is it a 'reserve.' It is a private printing press that Progressives of both parties have used to put citizens of The United States $20,000,000,000,000.00 (twenty trillion) in debt, to fund the build-out of a form of government prohibited by the U.S. Constitution.

This is some serious stuff.

In an even worse offense to the Constitution (if not outright treason), in that same year (1913) Wilson and his Progressives—or should I say, the Progressives and their Wilson—pushed through the Seventeenth Amendment, eliminating the "*Places of Chusing [sic] Senators,*" which the Constitution demanded to be "*by the Legislatures thereof.*" This codicil of the Constitution prevented interference with the balance of power between federal government and the States, and it was necessary to remove it before the nation could be taken over by them.

Each State's two senators were *required* to be chosen *by its legislature* to represent the States—not the people—and that particular element was so critical in the Founders' opinion, that this is actually the only thing in the Constitution that they prohibited from being changed.

After the passage of the Seventeenth Amendment, Senators became nothing more than extra Congressmen to be bought, sold and traded by the Progressives who quickly controlled them.

Wilson wrote, *"I am…forced to be a progressive, if for no other reason, because we have not kept up with our changes of conditions, either in the economic filed or in the political field."*[7]

President Wilson and the Progressives voided the principles upon which our nation was founded. The Federal Reserve, Sixteenth Amendment, and Seventeenth Amendment may rightly be called the Three Horsemen of the American Apocalypse. 1913 was the beginning of the end of our constitutional republic.

Wilson's *"changes of conditions,"* destroyed the balance of powers in favor of centralized, concentrated, all powerful bureaucratically-controlled federal government and provided it with unlimited funding by hocking our nation's future to the bankers who controlled him.

But here we are a century later, and we finally have a chance to bring control of our nation back to rule of law and Constitution. By an amazing turn of fate, the first president in decades willing to stop these people is in the Oval Office. Love him or hate him, if you love your country as it was designed, you need to get on board, 'cause he's probably our last chance.

I believe he could and just might end their control by simply enforcing the contract of every federal employee. Each of these Progressives now

---

[7] *Rediscovering Americanism: and the Tyranny of Progressivism,* by Mark R. Levin, p. 56. Threshhold Editions, New York, July 2017.

running our government took an oath to faithfully uphold the U.S. Constitution which is nothing more than a contract between 'us' and 'them.' If our contract says all men are created equal and must be treated that way under law, it is their sworn duty to live by that premise and insure its implementation in everything they do—or leave government. It is final. No special powers, treatment or protections are allowed, unless equally shared by all Americans—which at present is far from the case—and 'they' cannot exceed the Constitutional authority we granted federal government without also violating their oath to uphold the contract.

Just imagine the results of holding all government employees accountable to their oath of office. There would be no more self-granted immunity for judges and prosecutors who knowingly violate the constitutional rights of those citizens who come before them to fill the American prison factories. No more sweetheart retirement and healthcare deals for members of Congress and government employees, if *We the People* don't have them as well.

No more unelected bureaucrats creating laws under which we must live and then selectively enforcing them only against their enemies. No exceptions allowed, and all unlawfully-connived statutes of "Administrative law" are immediately void.

Our contract states that these officials and employees derive their powers solely from us—*We the People*—through our elected representatives, and that relationship can not be changed without our explicit permission. That is also final. Those who refuse to follow these rules must be terminated.

So if the president issued an order as Executive requiring each of his department heads to review every employee for compliance with their oath of office—and terminate those who had violated it—that would more or less empty Washington, DC of Progressives. Upending constitutional government is their clearly stated core goal and any overt act in subversion of the document they swore an oath to uphold is adequate cause for their termination.

There is no *progress* under this bankrupt philosophy. 'Progressives' can only take us backwards to a time that preceded our first *revolution* in 1776. Back to a time when one class ruled the other and there was no pretense of equality between them. Back to a time when individuals had no rights or protections from the elites who ruled them, as is precisely the stated goal of so-called 'progressives' today. It is Elitism, plain and simple. *"I'm better than you. I'm smarter than you. I should be the benevolent dictator of your fate....and you must trust your fate to me, rather than believing in yourself. I know better what is good for you than you do—or those you might choose to represent you."*

Yep. It's time for the second revolution—back to our own way of government rather than the Progressive Elitism of the past century that has nearly destroyed us.

Progressive! What a joke. This philosophy is as old as any other form of slavery or feudalism. It's just been repackaged as something positive and sold to people who can't think for themselves by billionaires like George Soros and Jeff Bezos, but it is poison for the human soul—and the end of true freedom. *"The New Freedom,"* President Wilson? It sounds very much like "the Old Serfdom" to me.

The ultimate game is the same as it has always been—use law and force to put one class of heavily protected elites over the other class or classes, denying them means of defense or the freedom to speak out against their masters without severe consequences.

The strangest part of it all for me is that the Progressive billionaires funding domestic terrorist groups such as Antifa and violent rioters like Black Lives Matter are using the very people they will put back in the yoke first as their fighter pawns on the streets. And instead of tearing down the statues of real racists like Progressive founder Woodrow Wilson, they are tearing down those of the men who gave them the rights and powers to be free to do what they are doing.

Is it too late? Perhaps not. We finally have a leader with the courage to take them on, or I would not have wasted my time writing this book on how to do it. This is a very specific game plan for restoring constitutional governance, but it is no good without a coach and team willing to put it on the field. President Trump is one hell of a coach but he is currently having to run every ball himself. No guards or tackles in Congress protect him. He's a quarterback with no ends or backs to help him score, and they are allowing the deep state Progressives—still in government— to pummel him.

So it is not only important, but critical, that we get the president a team. I don't care if they are sensible Dems, Independents, or even Republicans who actually vote as they promise, but no more Soros-funded Progressives who have declared war on our Constitution. The 'Progressives' of both parties must go.[8]

Given the hostility against Donald Trump by the leadership of his own party, it is hardly surprising to find that Progressive billionaire, George Soros, is now buying the Republican leadership as well. Senator John McCain of Arizona, Republican Speaker of the House Paul Ryan, former Republican Congressman and present Governor of Ohio, John Kasich (who is making noise about a run against Donald Trump for Pres-

---

[8] Hungarian billionaire, George Soros, (born György Schwartz; August 12, 1930) is worth an estimated $23 billion, though it has never been disclosed how he went from young, Jewish, Nazi collaborator/ informant to one of the world's richest men following World War II, other than suggestions that his adoptive Nazi father—whose job was taking wealth from Jewish captives—did not turn it all over to his Nazi masters. Soros identified his neighbours and fellow Jews in Budapest to curry favor with the Nazis, many of whom were sent to death camps. As he admitted in his 1998 interview with *60 minutes* (https://www.youtube.com/watch?v=QSyczwuTQfo) when asked if he had any regrets for what he had done to them, he answered, "No, not at all." Soros is an avowed atheist who recently pledged $18 billion to fund domestic terrorist groups and organizations (such as Antifa and BLM), and is currently funding the caravan invasions by MS-13 gang members and migrants from Central America through the southern borders into the United States of America, using the front of two Catholic charities. Soros has also pledged these funds in support of organizations whose goal is to bring down duly-elected American president, Donald J. Trump.

ident in 2020); Senator Marco Rubio of Florida, Senator Lindsey Graham of South Carolina, and Congressman Carlos Curbelo of Florida were at one point in Soros' progressive pocket and on his payroll. Some still are.

Officials and politicians who take money in exchange for adopting Progressive goals should be impeached for violating their oath of office as well because they also swore to uphold our Constitution. If taking Progressive anti-Constitutional positions was a requirement of getting Soros/Bezos cash, they must go. They can either uphold the Constitution as they promised, or they can tear it down in exchange for billionaire cash, but they should not be allowed to have it both ways.

The Progressive ideology is evil incarnate and offends every principle that once made our nation great. We cannot make America great again until this poisonous reptile is punished or banished from our land. Progressivism in itself is a criminal ideology as it is committed to debasing our chosen form of government and establishing an unelected ruling class. I certainly am not suggesting going back to McCarthy-style hearings, but treason to and under our Constitution is actually one of the three valid crimes federal government is authorized to punish.

Let these elitist say anything they want under their right of free speech, but each overt act of subterfuge to our Constitution should be punished severely. It is treason, and playing God with our freedoms and lives is not acceptable. Does that also sound too harsh?

On August 21, 2016, Soros wrote, "*I fancied myself as some kind of god … . If truth be known, I carried some rather potent messianic fantasies with me from childhood, which I felt I had to control, otherwise they might get me in trouble.*" (`https://yournewswire.com/george-soros-i-am-a-god-i-created-everything/`)

That is the ideology this former Nazi informant and robber of Jewish wealth espouses, and he has no regrets. "*It is a sort of disease when you*

consider yourself some kind of god, the creator of everything, but I feel com-fortable about it now since I began to live it out." If this man is God—as Progressives are actually taught to consider themselves if they want to be an Elite rather than a 'deplorable,'— then the Devil must be out of work.

Recent history and news has proven that the entire top tier of the FBI, the IRS, the DOJ, the DHS, the DNC, its admitted controllers (the Clintons), and so many other Progressives—both Democrat and Republican—are trying to play God like Daddy Soros too. They are now known to have taken part in a conspiracy to depose a duly elected president, yet none of them have ever (yet) faced the penalties and ruin they have so wantonly dispense against their enemies. It's time for them *all* to pay the penalty—including their Progressive god in New York—Big Daddy Warbucks—George Soros.

Like him or hate him, Donald J. Trump is perhaps the only man capable of fixing this mess. He is beholden to none and doesn't have to prove anything to anybody except those who voted for him (and he is on fire to do that) so I hope everyone will give the man a chance to stop the Progressives before they have completely destroyed our nation.

They are the real enemy, not President Trump.

Action Plan

The first step is to educate yourself on how this happened. There is no better place to start than *The Creature from Jekyll Island: a Second Look at the Federal Reserve,* by G. Edward Griffin. First published in July of 1994, this book is now in its fortieth printing, over 20 years later, which should give some idea of its continuing value and importance.

You may ask how a book about the Federal Reserve has anything to do with Progressivism and its drive to put our nation under the control of global Elites, but as has always been the case, money and power go hand in hand. Creating the most unaccountable printing press in the world where money could be created from the thinnest of air was the best way to achieve their political ends—and they have come very close to pulling it off. Had their Progressive queen, Hillary Clinton, won the presidency, the endgame would have been in play.

The next thing is to educate yourself about the man who may be the one to stop them—Donald J. Trump. Again, love him or hate him, but get it through your head that this is not a personality contest. This is war— war for the soul of our nation—and he is the only general we have who might be able to win it. So get the scoop on who he really is from the insiders who put him there. Second reading assignment is *Let Trump be Trump,* by Corey Lewandowski and David N. Bossie—the two guys who made it happen. They will not like everything I have written in this book—and may fight parts of it— but they know the man who can make it happen better than anyone and you will too after reading their story.

And finally, read Cambridge Professor Ha-Joon Chang's book, *Bad Samaritans: The Myth of Free Trade and the Secret History of Capitalism.*

This is the best book I've found on explaining the true intent of Progressives (a.k.a. Bad Samaritans) spreading the free trade myth for their own Elite benefit—and enforcing it through Progressive-run NGOs like The World Bank and The International Monetary Fund.

Chapter 2

TIME TO END THE MEDIA MONOPOLY

WHEN I read famous Washington Post journalist, Ben Bagdikian's, first edition of *The Media Monopoly,* he warned of the dire consequences of having just 50 media corporations controlling the content of public information and news in America. That was in 1983.

Fast forward, and as of 2018, over 80% of the world's information is controlled by *just five corporations*—Time Warner, The Disney Company, Viacom, News Corporation (Australia), and Bertelsmann (Germany). Add CBS and General Electric into the mix, and media watchdog groups such as The Waking Times have projected that 90% of the American media is now controlled by just six corporate giants. From 50, when Bagdikian first sounded the alarm—down to just six. This did not happen by accident. It was a clearly stated part of the Progressive plan, actually begun after they met in Jekyll Island, Georgia at J.P. Morgan's hunting club, and as part of the campaign for Progressives to get support to create their money machine—The Federal Reserve. They bought the leading newspapers in key regions that could make that happen—and it worked so well, they've been doing so ever since.

The five companies controlling most of the world's news, information, and all forms of media are so intertwined that they act more as one conglomerate than independent corporations—also by intent—because no real dissent can be tolerated in Progressive Utopia. These companies share cable systems, satellite channels, and even recording companies with a total of 141 joint ventures. These are business partners, not competitors.

When Bagdikian published the first edition in 1983, it was labeled (by the media) as 'alarmist' —but by the 20th edition published the year he died (2016)—his warnings paled in comparison to what had actually come to pass.

This ultra-liberal Pulitzer Prize winner saw the dangers of what was happening, even from within the camp of ivory-tower types perpetrating it. Bagdikian warned his adopted nation of America about the amorphous danger in allowing just 50 news companies to control the content, but it is now clear that when Regulators are controlled by Progressives rather than elected politicians (and sometimes even then), law is no object.

This warning came as Bagdikian—a journalist himself—was witnessing the devouring of thousands of independent information outlets into the 50 biggest bellies of a small handful of corporate beasts which had no interest in the locals they served. The number of information sources and voices being heard plummeted during his residency in the land of the free from those thousands of varying and contrasting views across the ideological spectrum (which had once engaged in vigorous debate in the public forum) to the five global players named in the opening of this chapter, controlling over 80% of world content in books, on radio, television, newspapers and magazines, as well as cable.

As a survivor of the Armenian genocide in his native Turkey, Bagdikian wrote that democracy—and ultimately, freedom itself—depended on an informed public exchange of ideas, unfettered and unrestrained by ideological suppression or monopolistic interests.

And here is the scariest part—the corporations controlling not only America's, but the world's news content, are owned and controlled by 15 of the world's wealthiest men and women—and all but one of them is a publicly self-proclaimed 'progressive.'

And get this—these extraordinarily wealthy Elites not only share ideology, they share management.

A study published by Columbia Journalism Review, as cited in Bagdikian's final printing (2016), revealed that News Corporation, Disney, Time Warner, and Viacom have 45 interlocking directors—forty-five—meaning in essence, the same people oversee the management of at least four U.S. branches of the world's media monopoly.

Convinced that conservative forces were behind this takeover of the world's information sources rather than the Progressives who were actually doing it, Bagdikian called—unsuccessfully—for the U.S. Department of Justice to enforce the monopoly laws against these giants until the day he died. No administration from that of conservative Ronald Reagan to liberal Barack Obama, however, had the courage (or nihilistic tendencies) to take on the media monopoly and break it up, though it was then clearly in violation of the existing ant-trust law(s) of several nations.

Perhaps we now have a champion with the courage to do it, but he needs a team that will follow the law rather than the billionaires funding its destruction.

We Are Now in the End Game

Information sources were intentionally consolidated by a small group of extremely wealthy individuals—just 15 of them today— with a view towards hegemony and control of content rather than competition, as evidenced by their shared management and resources. The plan was clearly to end competition, not just increase market share. Bagdikian's warnings were prescient. It was Orwell writ large, on an unimaginable scale. It was Sir Cecil Rhodes' plan of benevolent elites ruling the world in its endgame.

Today, the globalist media cartel ultimately decides who is heard—and more importantly—who is not heard, on our planet.

Should any entrant successfully run the gauntlet and become a meaningful bit player—such as Ted Turner did in his day, or more recently, Arianna Huffington—he, she (or it) will be quickly snapped up by the media monolith.

Welcome to the new world—which is becoming more and more like the Old World.

The Answer

Enforce existing laws. There is no need for a study group, a committee, congressional hearings, or anything that might allow a moment of delay. Anti-trust and monopoly statutes date back to 1890 in the United States (The Sherman Anti-trust Act) and exist in other nations as "competition laws." The Attorney General of the United States and his or her law enforcement equivalents around the world should immediately move to break up these giants by eliminating ownership of multiple means of communication by any one company or individual in any single market or across the spectrum of publishing, radio, film, visual—including cable.

Hungary, the home nation of former Nazi collaborator, George Soros, took a giant step in the right direction the week of May 13, 2018, by pressuring Soros' "Open Society Foundation" to leave Budapest and Hungary for good. Soros is moving his headquarters to Berlin—back to the roots of Bertelsmann and his other former Nazi allies in the media. Soros and the media monopoly's goal is to control the world's information, and therefore, the minds of its citizens, through propaganda rather than news.

This is a topic Soros knows well—as do his old allies from his Nazi days —Bertelsmann.

Other nations, including the United States, should follow Hungary's lead and eliminate this man's political influence machine and his attempts to undermine the freedom of their people and control their governments, while breaking up the media monopoly that supports his efforts to do so.

A Window of Opportunity?

There is one man alive today who is more reviled by the media monopoly than any other person in its history, and there is a reason. This man's name is Donald Trump, the president of the United States of America. The fact that Mr. Trump became president in spite of the cabal's maneuverings in opposition to it indicates that a brief window of opportunity may exist to end the monopoly's domination of the world's information sources.

I say Trump is the most reviled person in media monopoly history boldly because of the sad history of Bertelsmann—the European branch of the media monopoly—which willingly served Adolf Hitler's regime. Hitler should have been the most reviled person, but he is not. In fact, Adolf Hiler was Bertelsmann's best customer during the war years. The company printed 19 million books under The Third Reich, and thrived under Hitler's rule through large contracts to print anti-Semitic literature for the Nazi Propaganda Ministry, just as Jewish Nazi-Collaborator, George Soros, chose to work with them in his native Budapest, Hungary. You may think that is a mistake, but it is not. György Schwartz is his real name and at age 14, he switched from Jewish to Nazi Collaborator, selling out his Jewish neighbors and you will have an opportunity to hear him talk about in a few pages.

Bertelsmann's history would further suggest that the 'progressive' fathers of today's media monopoly may have had some measure of participation in putting Hitler in power, but they cannot dispute or claim that they did not make money off his cruel regime. They printed the propaganda necessary to keep him in power. Propaganda is a subject they know well and continue that practice now in service to the gods of Progressivism rather than Der Führer.

Whether one hates President Donald J. Trump or loves him is irrelevant. He is the only leader in a century who has nothing to lose by ordering his (next) Attorney General to bring the media monopoly back to rule of law and competition required of all businesses operating under it.

The President must press his Department of Justice (after its house-cleaning) to break up this handful of market monopolies just like AT&T was broken up by the Department of Justice in 1982. Time Warner, as example, should be dissembled into regional corporations, then further divided so as not to have cross-media control in any single market.

And what about Mickey Mouse? The Disney Company should be split into lots of little mice instead of the big Progressive Rat that tries to bend the minds of the world's youth. And so on. Bust them up and never let them coagulate again.

Our nation and the world could then get back to local news and local sources, reported by people who actually live there and care. Real reporting would quickly be revived and emanate from a wide variety of views rather than just one shrill voice that is ultimately controlled by 15 of the richest men and women in the world who are intent on selling the same dangerous message of progressivism to 80% of the globe.

It would be an ironic justice if President Donald Trump's legacy was bringing down the monopolistic forces which tried so desperately to destroy him (and America), would it not?

Action Plan

Personally I try to not let these monopolies enjoy revenue out of my pocket. I get my news online, and do not subscribe to CNN, MSNBC, CBS, and so on—but can still see it one day later (I live in Europe now). Mine is admittedly a small, inconsequential pocket, but if we collectively cut their revenue, it will have a withering effect that not even George Soros can afford to cover.

The next step is to press for the elimination of political PACs and even parties' power to buy their way into office by assaulting us with messages, as will be further discussed in the next chapter. There will be many against this idea but keep in mind that the Progressives control the biggest money printing press in the world and all we have is one billionaire.

By cutting off the means of the money to the media monopoly from political campaigns—except what the candidate him or herself can afford using donations only from their living, breathing constituents—a guy with a real message and a smart phone, like Donald J. Trump, can get elected.

We'll discuss the idea later…just please keep an open mind to it. Everyone can keep on lobbying and promoting good ideas, as they do now. All I want eliminated is the ability of corporations, PACs, foreign governments, and non-humans living outside of the district in question, to buy our representatives.

Chapter 3

I Want my Rep Back!

THE United States of America is a representative-style republic. It is not a democracy as mentioned in the Foreword. We have certain democratic principles, such as the popular election of members of the House of Representatives, but a democracy, we are not. We are a constitutional republic, designed to prevent mob rule that could reduce or eliminate guaranteed rights as the Progressives now seek to do through their version of 'democracy.'

We elect these representatives from within our respective congressional districts to do our bidding at the national level and to protect our interests so that we may go about our daily lives pursuing our visions of personal happiness, doing so with some reasonable level of domestic tranquility. The United States worked well like that for much of our history. The franchise of who was represented was improperly limited just to white men, but we have historical evidence that a constitutional America works extraordinarily well.

Today, in post-constitutional America, we find ourselves at the opposite end of the suffrage spectrum. Men and women of all colors, creeds, levels of income and education have suffrage (the right to vote), but it is no longer those living, breathing citizens who are represented in Washington.

What Went Wrong?

Rather than serving the people who actually live, work, and die in their congressional districts, most representatives now serve another class of citizen—the corporation. Legislation is overwhelmingly written on their order, and our representatives' activities, votes, and areas of interest, are based on those of corporate and pressure groups that fund them, instead of living, breathing constituents. That is the crux of our problems.

While it is still possible for a citizen to get assistance from his or her representative on mundane matters such as expediting the issuance of a passport, or perhaps getting some help in cutting through the bureaucratic red-tape at the local social security office, it can simply no longer be called a truly representative relationship.

Citizens have no real input or impact on matters of importance at the national level. Their interests, thoughts or opinions are of little consequence or concern to their representative, unless that particular citizen has the ability to write a substantial check to the congressman's re-election campaign. Even then, such influence is quite limited.

In 1874, the Supreme Court ruled in *Home Insurance Co. v. Morse*, that a "Corporation has the same rights to protection of laws as natural citizens." That one decision was a small beginning that soon started an avalanche of court decisions in favor of monopolists, oligarchs and corporate interests, which continues today. This imaginary class of citizen, the corporation, has in essence, robbed us of *our* representation.

Suppose you are in Congress and get two calls telling you to vote different ways on a piece of legislation. One call is from the out-of-state Chairman of a pharmaceutical company that donated over half a million to your campaign—as happened to one of mine—telling you to vote for legislation outlawing the use of natural herbs and remedies without a doctor's prescription (the original version of the bill actually tried to out-law even growing them at home). The other call was from—say me—a guy who had known you from college days, was a friend and even distant cousin, but tried to do everything possible not to use pharma products, only herbs from his garden.

Who is "Cuz" going to listen to? The Big Pharma bill was outside Congress's constitutional purview as was limiting a citizen's right to grow his own rosemary and thyme in his garden, but guess who got his vote?

And that is why no one should have the right to buy my rep's vote. Only those living, breathing human beings residing in his or her district should be able to donate money.

In a string of questionably garnered Supreme Court decisions, the real avalanche started with *Santa Clara County v. Pacific Railroad Co.* in 1886, but carried on through *Southern Railroad v. Greene* in 1910 and the rights of "citizenship" for these paper fabrications became cemented into American law. The court stated in all of these cases, "*Corporation is person within meaning of Fourteenth Amendment, which forbids state to deny to any person within its jurisdiction equal protection of laws.*"

These court decisions, taken directly from the United States Code, are attached as Appendix B. It is difficult to conceive of such a notion as corporate citizenship, until put in context, but then it becomes crystal clear that it was an outright fraud upon the nation, for which we are still paying the price.

As can be seen in Appendix B, the high court did not make this obtuse decision once or twice, but 14 times between 1886 and 1910 to insure that it could not easily be undone or overturned.

Giving a corporation citizenship is a bizarre and seemingly whacky concept until examined more closely, then you can see what an evil but brilliant Machiavellian ploy it was. It opened the doors for the monopolists and oligarchs to take control of the nation. For all intents and purposes, I suggest that has now been accomplished.

Why Did Corporations Want 'Citizenship'?

When corporations became citizens, they gained the right to donate to politicians. That was the reason for their vigorous pursuit of this status. Once established as law, the corporations were able to bribe politicians without an officer of the company going to jail for it, as had been the law from our beginnings as a nation. It was a crime for corporations, unions or special interest groups to donate to the campaigns of politicians prior to this decision, as they were not citizens. It was rightly called a bribe.

But no entity has the constitutional right to influence a congressman except a human being living in and/or registered to vote in that congressional district. The Supreme Court made corporate bribery legal back in the nineteenth century, and we see the results today.

For those naive enough to believe that the days of the robber barons and such corruption at the Supreme Court level are over, think again.

On January 21, 2010, the Supreme Court kicked out all stops on corporations, unions and PACs (Political Action Committees) being able to buy up politicians in its decision in *Citizens United v. Federal Election Commission*. Foreign corporations and governments can rent or buy our elected officials at all levels of government as well, so long as they stay within prescribed limits. This is not a Republican or Democrat issue, though the judges split along those lines, it is a freedom and sovereignty issue. Whose country is this? Does it belong to *We the People*, or *Them the Corporations*? At this juncture, the Supreme Court has said *"them"*.

A few feeble restrictions against such unconscionable bribery were established in 1990 and 2003 at the federal level, but those were gutted by the *Citizens United* decision, along with a 63 year-old congressional ban against corporate and union spending either for or against federal candidates. All restraints have now been eliminated, leaving the nation open for the death knell of our republic as it officially moves toward a corporatocracy.[1]

The very notion that paper boxes in a lawyer's office with some documents and a corporate seal have equal or greater political rights than a flesh and blood human being, while suffering none of the responsibilities of citizenship, is offensive. It is also morally wrong and unconstitutional.

Did our Founders Intend 'Corporations' to be Citizens?

There is not a single codicil or passage in the United States Constitution that mentions corporations or upon which such constitutional effrontery can be based. Corporate interests certainly cannot claim that such a notion was in the Founding Fathers' vision for the nation as their opinions were written.

Thomas Jefferson, the author of the Declaration of Independence and our third president, wrote: *"I hope we shall …crush in its birth the aristocracy of monied corporations which dare already to challenge our government to trial by strength, and bid defiance to the laws of our country."* Jefferson saw and recognized the potential dangers that have come to pass, even then in our nation's infancy.

The Constitution of the United States is not just some arcane document, it is a legal contract. It states the terms between the governed and government, and we were the grantors of its powers. The preamble to that contract is quite clear as to who are the parties to the contract:

---

[1]While I am uncertain who coined this term, I first saw it in a book by former insider, John Perkins, in his 2004 bestseller, *Confessions of an Economic Hit Man: The shocking inside story of how America REALLY took over the world.* Perkins confessed to being part of the team used by Progressive NGOs and global corporate giants who intentionally developed false economic studies to hook poorer nations into vast amounts of debt from Progressive NGOs and government (using their natural wealth as collateral), to get contracts for corporate giants and ultimately, to have the leverage to rob that nation of its natural resources when it could not pay back the money.

> *"We the People of the United States, in Order to form a more perfect Union, establish Justice, insure domestic Tranquility, provide for the common defence [sic], promote the general Welfare, and secure the Blessings of Liberty to ourselves and our Posterity, do ordain and establish this Constitution for the United States of America."*

Corporations are not mentioned in the entire contract. That is not from some oversight, as can readily be discerned from Mr. Jefferson's quote above. He wished them dead at birth. They simply had no business being involved in government's contract with its masters, "We the People," which is why they were excluded from it.

Adam Smith, whom many corporate CEOs would claim as the patron saint of capitalism, despised corporations, calling them *"a nuisance in every respect."* In his famous tome, *"An Inquiry into the Nature and Causes of The Wealth of Nations,"* he further claimed that corporations caused distortions of free economic activity and tied the *"invisible hand"* which properly allocated goods and services in a society. Apparently the misdeeds of corporations in England were the source of Thomas Jefferson's fear as well as Adam Smith's disdain of corporations' involvement with government. Of those merchant and manufacturing companies in England, Smith wrote they *"have extorted from the legislature... the greater part of our commercial regulations."* (Chapter VIII, Book Four, Conclusion of the Mercantile System). With corporate citizenship, they have extorted commercial regulations from our legislature in America also, which was exactly the idea of gaining citizenship.

The idea is to protect the established corporations in an industry by over-regulating it to prevent new entrants. It's also referred to as 'kicking away the ladder,' once a company has become dominant in a business. By making it hard or impossible for new players to start and compete—there is less or no competition.

Extortion, bribery and insatiable greed on the part of the corporate oligarchs, has been matched with the desire for power, position, authority and money on the part of those elected and appointed to serve us.

The deluge of corporate money being thrown at our representatives must stop completely. Only living, breathing citizens, who have the constitutional right and ability to vote for a candidate, should have the right to donate funds to his or her campaign. There should be no more soft money, hard money, political action committee bribes, or union dues diverted to buy special legislative favors. This must stop. We must take back our country, and we can never accomplish that if any entity above the individual can buy the loyalty of our representatives, including political parties. A representative's loyalty is constitutionally reserved for the men and women living in the district that representative was elected to serve.

We Can Fix This

This is probably the most important step in taking back our country, and it must be taken soon or the rest won't matter. It might also take care of the media problem, because the billions raised by these outside entities to buy elections ends up in the pockets of media monopolies. Without those funds, CBS, ABC, NBC, MSNBC, and CNN could not survive.

The Supreme Court has equated money with free speech, and I have no problem with that. But let me hear that box of papers utter just one word or even a syllable. Let me hear it speak. Let me hear it quote the Gettysburg Address or sing the Star Spangled Banner just once. I want to hear it shout for joy at the birth of its child, or weep at the loss of its son or daughter killed fighting for this nation.

Let me see that box of papers with its corporate seal show some sympathy for its fellow citizens rather than only seek a profit. Let me see it render service to its country rather than only to its shareholders. That box of papers is not one of us. It is not *We the People*, whose name is on our contract, The Constitution of the United States.

And it's dangerous giving them the reins to our nation. Every war fought in my lifetime seems to ultimately have been in service to those cardboard boxes and their corporate seals, rather than *us*. The corporate citizens don't have their own sons and daughters to send off to war to die for their raw materials, oil, or to seize foreign markets, so they have their pawns in government send ours. How many sons and daughters of members of Congress were deployed to Iraq, as example? Not a one.

This is only possible because these corporate 'citizens' can buy our representatives' hearts and souls with money. Would any honest Congressman vote to send our children to die for some corporate advantage or for barrels of oil that could be bought cheaper on the open market? The question answers itself and this tragedy must end.

Imagine for a moment what our nation's capital would be like if returned to constitutional government. Think of the People's City without the mob of lobbyists, lawyers, and money-changers clogging its arteries and our Capitol's hallways. Imagine 435 men and women quietly and diligently doing the business of their constituents, concerned only with their welfare, rather than being assaulted from dawn to dusk by groups from all over the world with bags of ready cash to buy *this* legislation or *that* favor.

What a difference it would also make in how they looked at their duties. Just think how very differently our representatives would vote on various issues if they could no longer take money from PACs, political parties or corporate-interest groups, but only from the individual citizens back home who elect them. My representative would have told the Pharma chairmen to take a hike and voted with me if he couldn't take the half a million in 'donations.' He'd have been more worried about getting trounced at the family BBQ back home—and not getting *my* $100.

Think also of the caliber of individual who might run for Congress, if it wasn't just an opportunity to get rich. Holding office would be in service to fellow man, rather than the brothel atmosphere of today where votes are sold to the highest bidders on issues having nothing to do with the lives and needs of those they were chosen to serve at home. If our nation returns to constitutional representation, each issue or piece of legislation would be weighed as to its worth to the folks back home rather than the amount of cash being given by a corporate donor. A far higher level of character and person would be attracted to the job of being a representative.

Monitoring for fraud could not be simpler. Voter registration rolls could be compared with the donor list of each candidate. If any names do not match, or the donor is not a permanent resident within the district, then fraud has occurred. The only exception to this would be military personnel or individual U.S. citizens from that district living in other nations, who were registered to vote there.

Until constitutional representation is restored where only living, breathing individuals have the right to contribute to candidates, we will not be able to take our country back. Without this step, we are destined to be little more than serfs in a modern-day feudal society, run by 'Progressive' corporations, parties, foreign interests, and PACs, which presently seem to control most of our nation's leaders—with one clear exception at the top.

While even more preferable that no contributions be allowed at all to stilt the representatives' views, this might preclude some good candidates without personal means of running for office from doing so. There is absolutely no constitutional context, however, for allowing groups, corporations, political parties, or even individuals who are not resident in the district to give money to someone else's representative. This is what has given corporations, PACs, unions, and foreign interests control over our representatives.

We must break the link between greed and power to save our nation. Our representatives must serve only us, the living, breathing citizens, who are party of the first part, *We the People*, in our contract with the United States of America. That contract is The Constitution of the United States. Nothing other than a human being with a beating heart can be recognized as *We the People* and have the right to vote—well, except maybe in Chicago.

Action Plan

Article I, Section 4 of the Constitution grants the state legislatures the power to prescribe the manner of election of both Senators and Representatives in their respective states. This is the ground where change can be made most effectively and expeditiously at this point in time.

At the State level we must press for legislation making it unlawful for any persons not resident in a Congressional district, or any group, corporation, PAC, union or political party to give to or spend money on a candidate. This will be fought in court, without doubt, but that will force federal courts and ultimately, the Supreme Court, to cite the provision in the United States Constitution which granted these other parties the right to purchase our representatives, which they cannot do. Such expansion of franchise was precluded by the Tenth Amendment.

At the federal level there is already a major campaign underway calling for a Convention of States. Article V of the U.S. Constitution gives states the power to call for such a Convention in order to propose amendments to the Constitution, when Congress refuses to do so. I say it's time we do it. It is clear that none of the Swamp creatures will, and we could really get some momentum if the president gets behind it, which I think he might. He's as frustrated as we are.

It only takes 34 states to call the convention and 38 to ratify any amendments that are proposed. The group leading for this call (Convention of States)[2] has limited any amendments only to those that, *"limit the power and jurisdiction of the federal government, impose fiscal restraints, and place term limits on federal officials."* This is an important factor (and reason for my support) because without such restriction, the Convention could be misused to expand federal power and reduce rights rather than rein in federal government and restore rights illegally taken from us.

The possibility of this actually happening has never been greater than today. In fact, as of May, 2018, the legislatures of Alaska, Arizona, Texas, Oklahoma, Missouri, North Dakota, Indiana, Tennessee, Louisiana, Alabama, Georgia and Florida have already passed COS Resolutions, and one chamber of the legislatures of New Hampshire, West Virginia, Virginia, North Carolina, Mississippi, Arkansas, Iowa, South Dakota, New Mexico, and Utah have approved COS as well. Legislation has been proposed for 2018 in Hawaii, California, Washington, Idaho, Wyoming, Nebraska, Kansas, Minnesota, Illinois, Kentucky, Ohio, Michigan, Kentucky, Ohio, Pennsylvania, New York, and South Carolina.

That's 39 States that have already passed COS or are in the process of doing so. If your state is in process, let your voice be heard (see website address in footnote of the previous page). If COS legislation has not yet been proposed in your State, please contact the Convention of States and volunteer to help their efforts.

George Soros declared war on the Convention of States in mid-April of 2017 (Good Friday, no less—an odd choice for an avowed atheist) announcing the formation of the largest radical left alliance in U.S. history to oppose it. Funding has been offered to *"almost every radical, liberal, progressive, Marxist group in America."*[3] Sixty-six of the most liberal

---

[2] https://conventionofstates.com. The petition can be signed at this site.
[3] https://conventionofstates.com/opposition

(progressive) groups trying to bring down the U.S. Constitution and our president have signed up for funding by Soros in exchange for fighting this Convention....and Hillary Clinton is their spokeswoman.

The fact that the billionaires funding the Progressives are so violently against this constitutionally authorized plan to rein in our bankrupt nation—and Hillary Clinton is their spokeswoman—should be enough reason to support it.

Chapter 4

FIX THE SEE-SAW—
RESTORE BALANCE OF POWERS

THE key provision of original constitutional design to prevent federal government from ballooning into the tyrannical, bureaucratically-controlled mess it is today was the mandated method of electing U.S. Senators—though few know it.

Article I, Section 3 of the U.S. Constitution states: *"The Senate of the United States shall be composed of two Senators from each State, chosen by the Legislature thereof, for six years; and each Senator shall have one vote."* [Emphasis added]

In other words, Senators represented the sovereign States rather than the individuals living in them, as briefly discussed in the Foreword.

As long as this mandatory method of choosing Senators was followed, there was only so much mischief and damage federal government could do. The United States Senate was a serious deliberative body of leaders, chosen by the elected leaders of the States themselves, to protect the sovereign interests of each State from an expansion of federal powers beyond constitutional limits.

And this key piece of the design worked. Any senator who did not sufficiently defend the rights of his sovereign State against attempts by the federal government to usurp its powers (or spend its money), would quickly find himself removed and replaced by someone who would.

We Were Warned

Thomas Jefferson foresaw what might happen without such a provision, and firmly advised James Madison on the dangers the nation would face. He wrote: *"I do verily believe that if the principle were to prevail of a common law being in force in the United States (which principle.... reduces us to a single consolidated government), it would become the most corrupt government on earth."*

Jefferson also wrote, *"Our country is too large to have all its affairs directed by a single government."* When one considers there were only 13 sparsely populated colonies with 90% of the entire nation's population living within 25 miles of the Atlantic coast when those words were written, their relevance today becomes even greater.

It was removing representation of the States that reduced us *"to a single consolidated government,"* and it was tinkering with the delicate design and balance between State and Federal power that upset that vision and balance.

The Senate—the protectors of limited federal government—are now the biggest proponents of 'a single consolidated government' and have consistently voted since 1913 to expand its scope rather than protect the loose federation of nation-states joined together for open trade, single currency and joint defense, as was their Constitutional purpose.

The population of the United States is now well over 300 million, with 50 states stretching from Maine on the North Atlantic, to Hawaii in the middle of the blue Pacific. The need for more localized, less centralized, governance, as Jefferson recommended, has never been greater.

This is the One Thing That Could Never be Changed, But They Did

The framers of the Constitution were so strongly wedded to the election of Senators by the State legislatures that they put this protective mechanism out of bounds to change in Article I Section 4. Congress was allowed to alter the State's regulations regarding elections in many ways, "*except the Places of chusing [sic] Senators.*" That was not subject to change, and was specifically and clearly intended to always remain the province of, and to be carried out in, the legislatures of the respective States.

The confluence of money from the new corporate citizens, and their agenda of seeking national monopolies, persuaded Congress to violate government's contract with *We The People* in the form of the Seventeenth Amendment to the Constitution.

The proposal was promoted as a 'progressive', *democratic* idea, and became law on May 31, 1913. It also acted to remove our protection against the expansion of federal power, just as feared by the nation's Founding Fathers—and sought by the Progressives.

As President Woodrow Wilson later said of these terrible deeds which he helped put in place at the orders of his banker-backers, "*I fear I have sown the seeds of my own nation's destruction.*" Wilson was correct. He had done just that. The United States of the Constitution was debauched and hobbled in service to those who put him in power to do so.

The Seventeenth Amendment changed our Guardians of Limited Government to nothing more than congressmen at large, with little loyalty to rights of State or constituents.

The Seventeenth Amendment Violates the Constitution

The Seventeenth Amendment reads:

> *"The Senate of the United States shall be composed of two Senators from each State; <u>elected by the people thereof,</u> for six years; and each Senator shall have one vote."*

Amnd. XVII [Emphasis added]

That clearly violated the Founding Fathers' prohibition against changing the place of choosing when passed, which should also render it null and void if challenged.

While the idea of popular elections for Senators of the States was appealing on an emotional, populist level, the very purpose of the U.S. Senate was negated by so doing. These congressmen at large could be bought and sold by the moneyed 'progressive' interests and corporate citizens just as their counterparts in the House of Representatives had been since the Supreme Court decisions improperly gave corporations the right of citizenship—which was why it was done. It was far more difficult to buy off someone elected by the leaders of a nation-state—until he wasn't.

Before Amendment XVII, Senators were the guardians of constitutional balance and provided the much-needed restraint on federal government exceeding its limits of power. The House of Representatives represented the People, while Senators represented the Sovereign States.

By eliminating this key component of design, power and money immediately flooded to Washington, DC and it has never slowed or stopped since.

A visitor to the nation's capital can visually mark the time-period of the beginning of the republic's demise with a short walk to Georgetown, where everything appears to have sprung up in the same era and epoch. That is because most of it did.

At the turn of the 20th century, it was still customary for members of Congress to live in boarding houses while serving their term, and few of them wanted more than one. With the assistance of a secretary, they tended to the business of their constituents, often slogging through muddy streets to do so. Few wives joined their men in the nation's capital. It was an unpleasant place to be.

As Congressman Albert Gallatin of Pennsylvania once wrote of Washington, DC, "*The Federal City is hated by every member of Congress without exception of person or parties.*" That was true because power and funds of federal government were very limited, as intended by the founding fathers, and there was none to waste on unneeded amenities. That was also by *design*, and no Senator would allow that scope to be expanded unless it was absolutely vital. That is because revenue for federal government was derived from "*Taxes, Duties, Imposts, and Excises*"[1] on goods coming into the country and luxury items, but any shortfall was paid by the States on an allocated basis depending on their population, which is why the Census was established in the Constitution to be taken every 10 years.

By voting to expand federal government, the Senator would be forcing the legislators *who elected him* to raise revenues from the citizens *who elected them* to fund it—which could have serious political consequences. Such a spendthrift Senator would find himself home and out of office rather quickly.

With the brakes removed from the federal locomotive by the passage of the Seventeenth Amendment (combined with the other unconstitutional acts of 1913 that allowed federal government to tax the people and print valueless paper money) the streets of the nation's capital were soon paved with gold, though it was fool's gold to be sure. The DC party was on and it has never stopped since.

The Wages of Sin....

The Great Depression—which was brought on by this excessive printing of fake money—was the first hangover from that party, but by then, fash-

---

[1] Article 1, Section 8, Clause One of U.S. Constitution

ionable townhouses, bars, restaurants and brothels covered the empty knolls around Foggy Bottom. Hotels were built and filled with wealthy interests buying favors from the nation's elected representatives—which included Senators freed from bondage to home-state and constituent interests.

Being a Senator changed from public service to a lucrative career for those who could buy or have their way bought into the game and the formerly sovereign nation-states were no longer represented in federal government. The damage has been immense.

Senate staffs ballooned from one to 21 over the ensuing decades and wives, girlfriends (and boyfriends) rarely wanted to stay home any longer. DC was the place to be.

But with every dollar taken from *We the People*, and with every power usurped by federal government or constitutionally unauthorized law passed by Congress, *We the People* correspondingly suffered an equal reduction in potential income, right of self-governance, and level of personal freedom.

The Founding Fathers knew exactly what they were doing placing the upper house of Congress as a protective body and mechanism against such federal power. Correspondingly, the progressive oligarchs knew precisely what they were doing by paying to have that protection removed from the Constitution and taxing the income of the People so that federal power could expand. They were the beneficiaries of a 'single consolidated government,' which could be far more easily bought and controlled than 50 separate legislatures.

The IRS of today is little more than an armed revenue collector to fund this abuse, by robbing us of what we earn while Congress takes our rights rather than protecting them. The game continues through Congress distributing much of that booty and power back to corporate interests, war profiteers, professional unions and progressive monopolies that fund their elections—and round and round it goes.

Where Does All That Money Go?

For those who consider my assessment to be unduly harsh, I ask only that you review the federal budget for any year since and including 1986 and see where our money has gone. Another meaningful exercise would be to study the annual reports from our own Freedom House Index, which was established in 1941 to rank totalitarian nations. By 2010, America fell from number One in freedom when the index began, to Forty-Third, falling behind many third-world nations and despotic regimes—and either by choice or force—Freedom House simply quit reporting America's place under President Obama.

Roughly one-third of the federal budget is now squandered on 1) undeclared wars abroad; 2) putting and keeping people in prisons for violations not under federal constitutional purview; 3) 16 unconstitutional spy agencies; 4) the so-called War on Drugs (better called the War on Civil Liberties); and 5) the equally unconstitutional Department of Homeland Security, which has done more to reduce the security of our freedom from government tyranny than anything in our history.

No one knows the NSA's budget for spying on us, but none of the items on the above list (including the NSA) are constitutional, wanted, or needed, and without them, the nation would have no deficit. If Senators still represented their States as designed, there would not be spending bills for $1.3 Trillion as were passed in March of 2018, and the alphabet agencies that drain our pockets and take our freedom would not be in existence.

How Deep a Hole Are We Really In?

This discussion of the problem of runaway spending created by the loss of State elected Senators should not avoid the elephant in the room, which is the national debt. The number is not just $20 Trillion as publicly stated— though that in itself is a lethal figure, as we can't even pay the interest on the interest—but that is just the *public* debt—money owed to bond and Treasury bill holders, largely foreign, who are now the nation's bankers. But what about the incredible $54 trillion borrowed from the so-called Social Security Trust Fund? I say "so called" because there is not one. Every penny of income ever paid into this illegally legalized Ponzi scheme has been spent on current expenses since the program began on August 14, 1935. There is no reserve.

This places the national debt at a staggering $74 trillion which is a number so large unless we restructure that there is no other expectation except a *crash and burn* scenario. No country has ever been close to such a debt. How bad is it? Just look at the public debt-to-GDP ratio and tell me how we are going to get out of this.

"At the end of the 2nd quarter of 2017, United States public debt-to-GDP ratio was at 103.8%,"[2] while 90% was considered the economic danger zone from which nations can rarely recover as recently as my years studying Economics at the University of Virginia.

Without President Trump in office doing everything possible to get our economy able to cope with its debt by expanding it and trying to limit the 'progressive' minefield of regulations preventing it, we would have zero hope.

I'm not sure that even he can do it due to the opposition he faces from the deep state progressives imbedded there—but at least now there is a chance, if we get him a team.

The U.S. is not the only nation that ever believed itself immune from the hard lessons of history and laws of economics, it is just the most recent one. It not only can happen here, it will unless we return to

---

[2] https://en.wikipedia.org/wiki/Debt-to-GDP_ratio

our design and put the brakes on Washington by making Senators once again beholden to their States—elected by their legislatures as required in our Constitution—AND NOT ALLOWED TO HAVE BEEN CHANGED.

What is the end game with unlimited debt? Perhaps the most reliable economic model of its effects I ever found as an economist was the most unlikely as well. Communist-era Russian economist Nikolai Kondrati-eff's[3] Long Wave Theory suggests debt will increase until the economy collapses, which he refers to as economic "winter." Debt must be washed out and its causes alleviated before the economic "spring" can begin, just as occurred during and after The Great Depression.

The U.S. Government's current spending path will put the nation in a perpetual economic Kondratieff *winter* from which it cannot escape, if not stopped now and reversed. You can't spend more than your debt service every year and hope to turn it back.

Put the Guardians of Liberty Back in Place.

Senators who represent the States' interests keep a leash on federal government, and we have seen what happens when that is not the case. Federal government will expand and usurp powers and duties never granted until it bankrupts the nation. That is why the component of States being represented in the original design, *could not be changed*, according to the Constitution.

With the Guardians of Limited Government still in place and elected by the State Legislatures as demanded, it is my firm belief that the long list of constitutional anomalies that have now brought us to economic ruin, could not have occurred. Senators, representing the States, would have prevented it.

---

[3] https://en.wikipedia.org/wiki/Kondratiev_wave

Things have not always been as they are today. The America even of my youth and the freedoms we had would seem unbelievable to my children. I hope to see it that way again before they have children. We should have stopped it sooner, but many did not know the changes allowed by or foisted on our grandparents were illegal. The sins of President Woodrow Wilson are only now being completely visited upon us generations later. But once we connect the dots and see what Progressivism has done, not acting to undo those evils becomes our own failure, and we can blame no one but ourselves for losing our country to them.

Let's Start by Teaching the Constitution Again.

The need for reintroducing American citizens to their own form of government has never been greater. Education is still the constitutional purview and province of the Sovereign States, though the federal agenda of the Department of Education has supplanted most if not all local content. Constitutional instruction is one of those important areas where States must reassert their authority to educate and teach citizens to have pride in their own State[4] and to be knowledgeable of their own rights and protections from federal authority and abuse, as well as their State's rights. Each young American should be taught about the nation's true form of government to prevent its further erosion to Progressivism.

For starters, they should be taught that we are a constitutional republic, where federal power is limited to a short and very specific list of duties, and putting the Senate back in charge of keeping federal government within its boundaries as their State's representative in Washington is only right.

---

[4]As a child, I remember studying the history of my own state and feeling the tingles up my spine reading of John Ashe, Speaker of the Assembly, marching his legislature to Cross Creek (now Fayeteville, NC) where they took the King's appointment Stamp Act broker hostage and with nothing more than their personal weapons, refused to allow Captain Black and his warship, the *Diligence*, to offload stamps for the new tax. Not a single stamp ever entered North Carolina. When home-schooling my own children in the 1990s, I tried to find these amazing books of State history, but they were gone. Millions of them were destroyed by the Department of Education—half were burned, and half were put in the landfill.

Action Plan

OK, the first step is education. We need to get the Constitution back in every classroom as they once were and make knowledge of that document and the rights with which *We the People* are imbued (including protections against tyrannical federal government) a part of every school's curriculum, and teach them the history of their own nation-state as well.

Adding the dissolution of the Seventeenth Amendment to the Convention of States agenda is key, and I have requested that addition of its president, Mark Meckler.

If the legality of the Seventeenth Amendment were challenged in court by a well-known constitutional organization such as The CATO Institute, based on its violation of the Constitution's prohibition against changing 'the place of choosing' it would certainly raise public awareness on the issue—and if the Supreme Court followed the Constitution (a bit of a stretch at this point to even hope for it)—we would win. Best to count on COS.

Until Senators are once again chosen in and by each State's legislature, the members of that body stand in violation of their oath to uphold the Constitution, and federal government is never likely to be restrained in its growth and usurpation of power.

Chapter 5

GET YOUR HANDS OUT OF OUR POCKETS!

GOVERNMENT, at the federal level has only been able to become so large, burdensome, powerful and over-reaching because of its unlimited source of revenue, even though that source was forbidden to it by the U.S. Constitution. That off-limits source of revenue was us, *We the People*.

In our contract with government, Section 9 of Article I, forbids any *"Capitation or other direct Tax"* to be laid upon the people. *"Government Taxes"* were to be derived from the respective States *"in Proportion to the Census or Enumeration hereinbefore directed to be taken"* as well as *"Duties, Imposts and Excises."* (Article I, Sections 9, 2 & 8, respectively)

The States with greater populations contributed more, while the less populous paid a smaller portion of the cost of federal government not covered by import duties, imposts and excises. Import duties also protected our nation's industries. This mechanism kept federal government lean, efficient, and out of our lives, by design, and during the period that America had the highest import duties in the world, it also became the globe's largest manufacturer—as proof that the free-trade myth is just that, a myth.

When Senators were still elected by the State legislatures as the Constitution requires, they would not allow legislation to pass at the federal level which would put an undue tax burden on the State government that elected them as explained in the preceding chapter. That would be political suicide.

Members of the legislature back home would view their Senator as having created a political problem for them if they had to raise taxes at the local level where they were elected, just to support a spendthrift federal government wasting money in Washington, DC.

It was a beautiful self-regulating design the centerpiece, as the reader now understands, being the election of the senators by the state legislators. They had very strong incentives to keep federal spending, power and growth, under tight control. If they did not, they lost their job representing their sovereign nation-State in Washington, DC.

Why They Did It.

The monopolists, oligarchs, 'progressives' and owners of corporations with national aspirations wanted control across state boundaries and at a national level. They could not accomplish that goal with a limited, fiscally-prudent federal government, in a country where each State made its own rules and requirements as to how corporations could operate.

While I have found no hard evidence this element of corporate restriction was part of any planned design, it did have a healthy, restrictive effect on powerful corporate interests. Any expansion into a new State required dealing with its unique laws and rules on a state-by-state basis.

The end of State sovereignty by passage of the Seventeenth Amendment hurt us, as there could not be such corporate hegemony if the States still held the upper hand in the balance of power.

The results of the tragic change can now be seen across the land. We have the exact same collection of box-brand purveyors of imported trinkets and junk food at every intersection in America, instead of thriving local industries and merchants. The corporate oligarchs of the 20th century knew that State authority controlling them must be removed and shifted to a more easily bought and controlled center. The District of Columbia became the place for one-stop shopping after the Progressives pressed for centralized federal power so their own could more broadly expand.

Before the curse of centralized federal power, States and local communities controlled their own destinies. If communities did not want local industries, merchants, restaurants and craftsmen destroyed by chains and store-brands from other States and nations, that was under their own control. There were no national chains or corporate interests before the cataclysmic changes in 1913 and the rise of federal power. After the Supreme Court overrode the Founders' intent and the Constitution in *Southern Pacific Railroad v. Santa Clara County*, out-of-state corporations could not be denied equal treatment under the high court's bizarre interpretation of the Fourteenth Amendment. Local cultures and economies were lost to this national hegemony and big corporate interests.

If an individual man or woman had the constitutional right to set up a small hardware store in another state, then a corporation from any state, could set up a large one, regardless of the detrimental effect it may have on the local economy. The view at every major intersection in the United States, whether it be in Allentown, Pennsylvania, or Albuquerque, New Mexico, is now the same as a result. Local cultures, producers, retailers, and suppliers, have all but disappeared.

The more powerful the national government could be made, the faster oligarchs, monopolists, and national interests could extend their financial empires and corporate stamp on the nation, crushing local enterprises and purveyors as they spread across the land under the guise of 'progressivism.'

This is a far cry from the humble capitalism envisioned by Adam Smith and his "invisible hand," and it could not have been accomplished without the onslaught of big federal government and control. What we have today is not capitalism, but a dysfunctional *corporatocracy*. The nation is ruled by politicians acting on the whim of large corporations and billionaire socialists and Progressives who want to destroy our nation's very design.

The only way they could insure their unlimited expansion was to create a powerful national government and environment where a *corporatocracy* could gestate and flourish. That required finding ways of reducing State power and supplying federal government with unlimited funding.

How They Accomplished It.

This lengthy introduction brings us to the Second Horseman of Apocalypse, the Sixteenth Amendment to the Constitution, whose passage, once again, directly violated a specific prohibition in the original Constitution against it, by imposing a direct tax on *We the People*, in breach of that contract.

When first researching this issue, two issues troubled me. Primarily, I wondered why monopolists, oligarchs and mega-wealthy men on the order of J.P. Morgan, John D. Rockefeller and Paul Warburg (the powerful men who prompted and largely paid for these efforts) would want an income tax, which they themselves might have to pay. That made no sense upon initial reflection.

The results of the income tax on that group, however, speak for themselves. As of 2018, a century after that federal income tax was put in place; there are 585 billionaires living in the United States. That accounts for 26.5% the world's total, though we have less than 5% of its people indicating that income tax has little if any effect on that top tier. A case could well be made that the destruction of these critical parts of our constitutional balance actually created the environment that allowed the present discrepancy and disparity of income between today's super-wealthy and the rest of us. *"The 400 richest American now have more wealth that the bottom 61 of the population."*[1] A GAO (General Accounting Office) study in 2008 revealed that nearly two-thirds of the corporations owned and controlled by this group of billionaires, paid zero income tax, even though their combined revenues for that year were in excess of $2.5 trillion.

Corporations as a whole contribute just 7% of federal taxes today, where, as recently as 1943, they contributed 40%. Approximately 90% of stocks, bonds, trust funds, and corporate equity are now owned by the wealthiest 10% of American society, according to the research of Professor G. William Domhoff of The University of California (Santa Cruz). More shocking, this same group who contributes so little now owns in excess of 75% of all non-home real estate as well. Progressive oligarchs and corporations not only control our government, but our country it seems, while contributing only a pittance towards its expenses.

But How Could it Have Happened?

This research led me to the inescapable conclusion that those powerful enough to coerce or bribe Congress and The Supreme Court into disavowing their sworn duty to uphold the Constitution, would have little trouble buying legislative protection for themselves against the consequences of those changes. That would be inexpensive child's play by comparison. Wealthy individuals carry a large percentage of the tax burden, but their corporations—where most of their wealth is now stored—do not.

---

[1] Institute for Public Policy report referenced in The Nation.
https://www.thenation.com/article/20-people-now-own-as-much-wealth-as-half-of-all-americans/

The anecdotal evidence and GAO statistics certainly support that theory. The corporate interests that benefit from and control 90% of the nation's wealth today contribute almost nothing towards its upkeep. This would have been impossible to accomplish without corporate citizenship, which allowed legalized bribery of legislators to enact changes favorable to them at our expense.

We the People got stuck with the tab in the form of the Sixteenth Amendment and its unconstitutional tax on our daily bread, while they eat cake. *We the People* versus *Them the Corporations*. Again, so far, '*them*' won.

The second area that troubled me greatly was why a majority of the public would have voluntarily supported such an illegal change in our contract. Why would we give federal government the power to dip its hand in our pockets any time it wished to do so? How could such a thing happen?

And that's where the story gets really interesting because—according to Supreme Court case, *United States v. Thomas*—it didn't. The Supreme Court's decision actually states "*Sixteenth Amendment is effective legal document, even though only four states ratified its language exactly as Congress approved it.*". [Emphasis added](See Appendix C)

So how did it become law of the land if the States altered the wording to avoid passage or refused to vote in its favor altogether? The law requires each State to *exactly* replicate the wording of an amendment in it's approval without change, or it is invalid.

They Did What?

The *Thomas* opinion justified this illegal act (and the court's refusal to address it) by stating that "*in 1913 the Secretary of State declared it adopted, and Supreme Court follows 'enrolled bill rule' providing that if legislative document is authenticated by the appropriate officials, that document is treated as adopted.*"

So according to the United States Supreme Court, all that is required to strip Constitutional protections according to their 'enrolled bill rule' is to say that an 'appropriate official' authenticated it, even if it never passed. Again, law is no obstacle when Progressives are in charge.

The actual breakdown of what happened can be found in Appendix C in *United States v. Foster*, where the numbers of discrepancies proven by the defendant were listed: "*of 36 states tendering Sixteenth Amendment ratifying resolution to State Department, 11 states had adopted versions with different wording, 22 states had altered its punctuation, and one state had actually rejected it.*" (See Appendix C, page 146)

Secretary of State, Philander C. Knox, lied about the Sixteenth Amendment's passage but the Supreme Court has chosen to take his word over the actual documents proving that it failed—and has banned further questioning of it.

From admitting that only four states properly ratified the Sixteenth Amendment in *Thomas*, the court made a subsequent ruling that effectively put a stop to any further questions, acting to end all challenges by claiming, "*Advancing argument, totally unfounded, that Sixteenth Amendment was not ratified by requisite number of states, will result in imposition of sanctions against taxpayer.*" (*Cook v. Spillman*). In another ruling, "*Validity of ratification of Sixteenth Amendment is now beyond review.*" (*United States v. Benson*).

Who Could Have Pulled Off Such a Thing?

So who was this Secretary of State, Philander C. Knox, who had the power (and protection) to lie to the nation about the passage of an unconstitutional constitutional amendment, without penalty? Who controlled him? No man could have the unbridled audacity to commit such an act of infamy unless he was absolutely certain he was backed and protected by the most powerful men in the nation if not on earth.

And he was. *Them the Corporations* had stacked the deck against *We the People* and Philander C. Knox was the dealer.

More specifically, Philander Knox was the Pittsburgh attorney who put together the world's largest monopoly of that day, U.S. Steel, for J.P. Morgan and Andrew Carnegie. He was the cabal's lawyer and architect of the massive merger of Carnegie Steel Corporation, based in Pittsburgh; Federal Steel Company, based in Chicago, the nation's largest; as well as National Steel, National Tube, American Steel and Wire, American Steel Hoop, American Sheet Steel, and American Tinplate. Soon after the merger, American Bridge and Lake Superior Consolidated Iron Mines were absorbed, and more the following year.

Knox was immediately moved to Washington, DC by the cabal to protect its interest and made Attorney General of the United States under President McKinley, where he stayed on under the cabal's next President, Theodore Roosevelt, to fight—monopolies. Not surprisingly, the largest monopoly in the world—his—U.S. Steel, was never touched, and the cabal went so far in 1920 as to garner a Supreme Court ruling that the company was not a monopoly, though there was none larger or more controlling in America for sure, and probably the world.

Knox then went into the Senate to help lay the groundwork for the corporate interests he served. J.P. Morgan and Paul Warburg had greater plans—making their Federal Reserve a bank to the world—on the U.S. taxpayers' nickel. Knox left the Senate to join their candidate, William Howard Taft, as his Secretary of State to promote "dollar diplomacy". This policy encouraged foreign borrowing from U.S. banks, as a prelude to the Federal Reserve, founded and owned by the same men that put these presidents in office.

Taft was not compliant enough for the Progressives' interest (though he was still their man) so Woodrow Wilson was brought into the race and nurtured by J.P. Morgan's agent, Colonel Edward Mandell House, who literally lived in the White House while Wilson was President. To assure Wilson's victory, former President Theodore Roosevelt was also brought back as a third party candidate (Bull Moose Party), to siphon off votes from Taft, which successfully put Wilson and J.P. Morgan's mole, Colonel Edward Mandell House, in the Oval Office.

Even President Wilson referred to J.P. Morgan's man as his *"co-President"* and made the statement, *"Mr. House is my second personality. He is my independent self. His thoughts and mine are one."*[2] Colonel House chose Wilson's cabinet, laid out his policies, and prompted him to enter World War I in spite of running for election as a pacifist, in order to protect the debt owed to J.P. Morgan by the British Government—which was losing the war.

By February 3, 1913, there was no one to stop them, and the law which never was—the Sixteenth Amendment—was declared law anyway by departing Secretary of State, Philander Knox, though only four States had properly ratified it by the Supreme Court's own admission in *Thomas*.

The Supreme Court has made it clear that it has no intention of following the Constitution or overturning this proven fraud. Attempts by individuals to do so have been wasted and, in fact, proven dangerous.

The researchers who compiled certified copies of each States' ratification documents and published them in a two volume set, *The Law That Never Was*, as example, were imprisoned, ironically, on tax charges, even after proving that the tax itself was illegal as the amendment allowing it never actually passed.

---

[2] *The Intimate Papers of Colonel House,* by Charles Seymour. (New York: Houghton Mifflin Co. 1926, Vol. 1, p. 114

Isn't There Still Something We Can Do?

I believe that the States whose documents prove they did not legally approve the unconstitutional amendment could still mount a combined legal challenge to the Sixteenth Amendment. The federal government has yet to figure out how to imprison a whole state, though I'm sure Homeland Security and the NSA would be working on it if such a challenge were made. Without the income tax, neither of those unconstitutional agencies could exist.

If federal government's power to rob *We the People* at will is ever challenged, the shrill cry from such agencies that live from this lifeblood of federal power will be fierce. Moans of gloom and doom will pour in from every power broker and beneficiary of this corrupt system, but that is nonsense.

Legal Sources of Revenue for Limited Government

Our contract gave more than adequate sources of revenue for a (limited) federal government to provide all the services it was authorized to perform. Federal income was derived from imposts (a tax on products or services), excise taxes (on things such as liquor, tobacco and luxuries), and most importantly, import duties, which protected American jobs and industries. These were the main sources of federal income and should all be re-imposed to replace the illegal tax on personal income.

Any shortfall was paid from the States, as mentioned, and as allocated by census—which is also why Senators prior to the Seventeenth Amendment staunchly fought against frivolous federal spending. That also acted to also limit mission creep, keeping DC within its mandate and limits of power. They would lose their jobs if the States were hit to cover huge deficits, as previously addressed.

So Tax the Corporations

There is no constitutional prohibition, however, against taxation on the income of *corporations*, as they are not individuals. Large corporations operating across State lines or national boundaries should be required to pay a federal tax. Taxation of corporations whose activities are limited to one State is a decision that each state should decide for itself.

For those who wish to hide behind the corporate veil and seek its protection or spread beyond the natural limits of human reach, let them pay a heavy toll for so doing. Not only would this limit the ability of large corporate entities to destroy small entrepreneurs and local companies, it would level the playing field and increase diversity of ownership in the economy. That is real homeland security, and once we have restored Representation to the People (Chapter 2), Congress can legislatively correct the court's gross misinterpretation of who is and is not the living, breathing 'citizen' as intended by Jefferson, Madison, and Washington rather than the corporate one which controlled Supreme Court Justice Waite, who let it happen.

A federal tax on large interstate corporations could fall under an excise or impost, without violating the letter or spirit of the Constitution.

As for import duties, they were intentionally put in place by our Founding Fathers and credit for that is likely due Alexander Hamilton. Many of Hamilton's suggestions in his 1791 *Report of the Subject of Manufactures*, such as subsidies and import bans, were deemed unconstitutional by James Madison, but not import duties, which have proven to work in two ways—legal federal revenue and protection of American industries.

The Intentional Lie of 'Free Trade'.

The United States held fast to its protectionist tariffs and import duties for 134 years before relaxing them in 1926. The vaunted Free Trade movement of recent decades is quite new. Free Trade has now destroyed most of our nation's domestic industries, while helping to further exacerbate disparity in incomes creating a class of super-wealthy. Free trade enriched them beyond imagination, as the GAO figures prove, while sinking the nation that supported them, into a quagmire of debt and unemployment.

It was not until America became the world's dominant economic power that it suddenly took up the mantle of Free Trade under the Progressives, just as Britain did as the world's leading economic force preceding it. History shows that Free Trade benefits the dominant economic power, but only those corporate interests that gain advantage from importing cheap foreign merchandise, or those making extremely advanced products which few other nations can produce— but it never helps the people. And under free trade, even those high technology jobs will disappear over time, and eventually, the manufacturing base will be gone, just as we now find ourselves today in post-constitutional 'progressive' America.

What good is saving a dollar buying a Chinese hammer at Home Depot, if there are no jobs left for *We the People* to earn the money to pay for it? Free Trade only helps *Them the Corporations*. The numbers don't lie. Free Trade neither works in practice or theory, except to the benefit of the free traders themselves.[3]

This is an Easy Fix. Go Back to Legal Forms of Revenue

Restoring an effective regime of constitutional import duties would not only provide a legitimate source of federal revenue to replace the 'capitation' tax on personal income, it would create the most dramatic boon

---

[3]Once again, I encourage you to read the best work I have found on this topic— *Bad Samaritans; The Myth of Free Trade and the Secret History of Capitalism,* by Cambridge Professor of Economics, Ha-Joon Chang (Bloomsbury Press, New York, 2008). I strongly suggest it as the best source for a full history of the myth of free trade.

to American jobs and manufacturing in the nation's history. Charging duties on imports would level the playing field once more and allow merchandise to be produced and purchased here, by people living and working in those same businesses.

There is no downside to exchanging the income tax for import duties except to the importers and purveyors of cheap goods. They have caused our staggering trade deficit and put our people out of work. Any increased cost of goods from import duties and higher costs of production would be offset by not paying income tax. The revived manufacturing base would also be a new source of tax revenue and jobs. Public support roles would plummet as manufacturing returned to our shores. Trump proved this in his first year in office.

One only has to look at the incredible improvement of the economy since President Trump's historic tax cuts in 2017 to see the economic effect of sensible policies. Unemployment dropped to 3.9% less than a half year after the tax cuts went into effect. Imagine if a small import duty were imposed on cheap and/or subsidised goods pouring into our nation from abroad—to level the playing field. America could begin making things here again, and what a boom it would be.

Small businesses—the kind that have historically produced 65% of the jobs in our nation—would begin springing up like mushrooms after a spring rain, all over our land. Communities would again have meaningful work, and the 'rust belt'[4] as it is now called across our northern states would again shine for all the world to see.

Historic American import duty rates would more than replace the revenue currently brought in by the illegal tax on personal income, and that revenue could easily support a *constitutional* federal government.

U.S. tariffs ranged between 40-50% until the First World War and were the highest in the world as far back as the Civil War. As Cambridge

---

[4]The region once known as The Steel Belt stretching from western New York to Michigan lost so much industry in the 1980s that it became known as The Rust Belt instead.

University economist, Ha-Joon Chang, wrote in his 2008 groundbreaking work regarding the "Free Trade" myth, *Bad Samaritans; The Myth of Free Trade and the Secret History of Capitalism,* "*Despite being the most protectionist country in the world throughout the 19th century and right up to the 1920's, the U.S. was also the fastest growing economy.*"[5]

Import duties not only protected American jobs, they allowed domestic industries to grow and prosper. They will again if we exchange 'Progressivism' for Trumpism.

No nation has ever free traded its way into prosperity. Not one. No nation has ever (voluntarily) become a free trader until its own industries matured or became competitive in the world economy.

Restoring federal government to constitutional sources of revenue would have a curative effect in place of the detrimental drag on the economy now caused by the personal income tax. This would also end the suffering brought to bear on individuals required to pay the income tax, shifting it to buyers of imported goods and luxuries instead.

Income tax is not only harmful to the nation, it is unconstitutional. It was foisted on *us* by outright fraud. There is probably nothing we can do about that unless the States who did not ratify it mount a suit over it. The Supreme Court has proven itself useless in correcting it, in service to big government and those who put them on The Supreme Court (as seems evident from the cases in Appendix C). It will once again be left to us to fix this in spite of our so-called leaders. They have become little more than minions for corporate and professional interests and monopolies—with one notable exception in the White House—and I again draw the reader's attention to the Convention of States as a means to roll government revenue back to its proper sources and uses. That appears to be our only way.

---

[5]Ibid.

Federal government's ability to pick our pockets must end or our nation and what's left of our freedom will. That's the choice. Government will only remain limited as long as its sources of revenue are *limited* as well.

The answer lies in taking back our representatives from their corporate masters as discussed in Chapter 2, and forcing them to legislatively undo this constitutional anomaly of a tax on income by calling for a Convention of States to undo it.

Action Plan

Let's start again with a homework assignment. If you didn't order this book *Bad Samaritans; The Myth of Free Trade and the Secret History of Capitalism*, by Cambridge Professor of Economics, Ha-Joon Chang when I suggested it before, please do so now. You have to read it to put this Free Trade nonsense in context. You will see that there is absolutely no danger in doing away with the income tax and relying on legal revenue means like import duties. Sure, the multinationals and Progressives will scream, cause they're the (only) ones benefitting.

As President Trump has already begun doing on steel and aluminium products, we should reinstate constitutional sources of revenue, beginning with imposts, excise taxes and especially these import duties on all products other than perhaps some raw materials, coming in to our nation. That will have the immediate effect of rebuilding our domestic industries and returning jobs to America. As the income tax is phased out, any revenue shortfall can be allocated to the States—if needed—to fund legitimate federal government expenses, as provided in Article I, Section 2 of the Constitution.

Support only candidates who agree to support a Convention of States, so the 'Law that Never Was' (the Sixteenth Amendment) can be eliminated in spite of court and government.

We must also begin grassroots campaigns to pressure State governments that did not properly ratify the Sixteenth Amendment to challenge its legality and legitimacy in federal court.

Counting just three defects, 1) Not ratified by state legislature and so reported, 2) Not ratified by state legislature, but reported as ratified, 3) Missing or incomplete evidence of ratification, but reported as ratified; the Amendment failed by 13 States.

When all defects that require nullification are included,[6] only two States credited with approving the amendment did so according to those requirements.

As sovereign members of the Union, States could not be attacked for bringing suit against federal government for its provable fraud (as individuals have been) but only a legal challenge would be effective at this juncture, brought to court by any of the 34 States that did not properly ratify, as can be seen at www.thelawthatneverwas.com.

A final step that could be taken at the State level is to impose income taxes on large corporations, but only those that reach across State or national boundaries to level the playing field and protect small businesses and entrepreneurs who provide most of the jobs in America, while keeping them competitive with the larger corporations and multi-nationals that have nearly destroyed them.

---

[6]"The authority usually cited for the criticality of ratification without errors of spelling, capitalization, or punctuation, is from DOCUMENT NO. 97-120, of the 97TH CONGRESS, 1st Session, entitled How Our Laws Are Made, written by Edward F. Willett, Jr. Esq., Law Revision Counsel of the United States House of Representatives, in which the comparable exactitude in which bills must be concurred under federal legislative rules is detailed:

Chapter 6

STOP THE COUNTERFEIT MACHINE

IN the watershed year of 1913, the Third Horseman of the Apocalypse of our republic appeared in the form of the Glass-Owen Act. It was better known as the Federal Reserve Act, though what it created was not federal and it certainly was not a reserve. In fact, it was quite the opposite. It was a private central bank, owned by the world's wealthiest individuals, who were granted the power to print currency without any backing, outside of law and in violation of the United States Constitution.

It was a license to create money of no real value, to fund the growth of federal government beyond all natural economic and constitutional limits, at a tidy profit to its private owners.

This was not the United States' first experiment with what is kindly called *fiat currency* (money of no real or intrinsic value)—it was the fourth— a little-known fact.

The other attempts at circumventing constitutional requirements for legal tender all ended in disaster. The Federal Reserve may cost us our nation altogether. The hole the private bankers dug for us this time may be too deep to crawl out—but there is a solution if we end it while Donald Trump is president.

The Outcome is Always the Same

The Federal Reserve has for all intents and purposes, already caused the nation's bankruptcy. Congress discharged *all* debts not payable using *Federal Reserve notes* on June 5, 1933, and it became law (House Joint Resolution 192). The nation could no longer pay its obligations. This took only 20 years to occur under the monetary authority of The Federal Reserve (1913-1933). The United States has, in essence, been under Chapter 11 bankruptcy ever since. Gold ownership was suspended, and all legal debts "*heretofore and hereafter incurred*" could only be paid in fake money (federal reserve notes) of no real value rather than constitutional, gold or silver backed notes, which still existed until 1964.

It is key to our understanding that central banks *are not for the benefit of the nation's people*, as history has proven. They *are for the benefit of those who own or control the central bank*, and the political/financial elite they serve—in our case—the government Progressives who founded it—and those who control them—the Progressives who benefit from it.

The first central bank in America was chartered by the Continental Congress in the spring of 1781, before the Constitution was drafted. It was called *The Bank of North America* and was fraudulent from the start. When its founder, Robert Morris, couldn't raise the initial capital ($400,000), he used his political influence with his former employee, Alexander Hamilton, to make up the difference. Morris was allowed to take gold the United States borrowed from France, and deposit it into his new bank. He then created *fiat* money against the debt (not the gold), which he loaned to himself and his associates for the required cost of subscription in the bank.

By 1783, just two years later, it was shut down by President George Washington. This failure, combined with the nation's pre-revolutionary experience with the un-backed *Continental* dollar, led to the constitutional prohibition against such currency of no real value in Article I, Section 10.

The crisis precipitated by 'the Continental' was still fresh on the nation's mind when the Constitution was written. Due to that failed national currency and the States' own un-backed currencies, inflation reached 5,000% between 1775 and 1779. This eventually happens to all such *fiat currencies*, including the Federal Reserve notes of today.

In 1779, George Washington wrote, "*A wagon load of money will scarcely purchase a wagon load of provisions.*" In a letter to his friend and revolutionary general from France, Lafayette, George Washington wrote:

> "*We may one day become a great commercial and flourishing nation. But if in the pursuit of the means we should unfortunately stumble again on unfunded paper money or any other similar species of fraud, we shall assuredly give a fatal stab to our national credit in its infancy.*"

In spite of these experiences and failures, Alexander Hamilton was back in 1790 with a proposal for a second private central bank, incorrectly named, *The First Bank of the United States*. It was operational by 1791, but again employed the same fraudulent capital scheme as its predecessor, by borrowing government money to pay the capitalization. The bank's biggest critic, among many, was Thomas Jefferson. He publicly called Hamilton's hand on the fraud, declaring, "*Call it by what name you please, this was not a loan or an investment, but an outright gift.*"

As is always the case with un-backed or fractionally backed currencies, wholesale prices rose by 72% in the ensuing five years and public outcry began against it. The charter was not renewed in 1811, and the nation's second central bank was closed.

Undaunted, the financial schemers and money-changers were back by 1816 with another plot. Congress chartered *The Second Bank of the United States*, (though it was America's third).

Again, inflation spiked and the economic roller-coaster that always attends such un-backed currency tormented the nation until President Andrew Jackson put an end to it. He ran for re-election in 1832 on the slogan, *"Bank and no Jackson, or no bank and Jackson."*

Jackson won and the charter was not renewed. The nation then entered an unparalleled era of real prosperity which lasted until the National Bank Act of 1863 created not one, but many, nationally-chartered banks, to print unbacked currency for the War Between the States.

In a private letter to William F. Elkins on November 21, 1864, President Abraham Lincoln wrote of the money power he helped to create:

> *"The money power preys upon the nation in time of peace and conspires against it in time of adversity. It is more despotic than monarchy, more insolent than autocracy, more selfish than bureaucracy. I see in the future a crisis approaching that unnerves me and causes me to tremble for the safety of my country. Corporations have been enthroned, an era of corruption will follow, and the money power of the country will endeavor to prolong its reign by working upon the prejudices of the people, until wealth is aggregated in a few hands, and the republic destroyed."*

President Lincoln's dire predictions have come to pass in full. The rapacious takeover of the nation by corporations was a *fait accompli* within decades of Lincoln's murder. Taking control of the nation's currency via The Federal Reserve was the *coup de grâce* and death of the American republic for all practical purposes.

The Results are in, and They are not Good.

Money and power continued to collect in fewer and fewer hands just as Lincoln predicted, throughout the following century. By 1979, the top .1% earned 20 times the income of the bottom 90%. By 2006, that disparity between the richest .1% and the bottom 90% had grown to 77 fold.

The nation, today, *"is in a few hands, and the republic destroyed,"* just as Lincoln feared it would be. The corporations have *"been enthroned"* by the Court as 'citizens', no less, and our currency is under their private control.

This could not have happened with constitutional money of real, intrinsic value. It grows organically and steadily, and does not lend itself to concentrations in the hands of few in a free nation.

The United States Constitution authorized the federal government *"To coin Money,"* and *"fix the Standards of Weight and Measures"* in Article I, Section 8 and Article I, Section 10 specifically prohibits the sovereign States from making *"any Thing but gold and silver Coin a Tender in Payment of Debts."* There are no exceptions. All four of America's central banks have been nothing more than ploys by men of extraordinary wealth and the politicians they controlled to circumvent the United States Constitution for personal gain or unlawful expansion of federal government and power.

The Game and How it is Played

The concept of central banking is quite simple. Since government cannot legally make worthless cash under the Constitution, Congress authorized its wealthiest donors to do so and they were paid handsomely for it. Congress has mandated that the fraudulent cash must be legal tender for payment of debts, in direct violation of the passage cited above from the United States Constitution, requiring only gold or silver.

The worthless cash is of value only because no other means of exchange is allowed—by force of law. Direct access to newly printed currency is limited to government, large Progressive banks, and large Progressive corporations when it initially enters the economy. Every additional bill printed as the money supply is expanded, reduces the value of every one already in existence, and they all become worthless as time goes by.

As Eighteenth century French writer Francois-Marie Arouet Voltaire wrote, "*Paper money always returns to its intrinsic value, which is zero.*" If $10 are in circulation and one more is added, each one of the existing dollars becomes worth only $.90, and so on. Throughout the Administration of "Progressive" President Barack Obama, the Federal Reserve created approximately $1 trillion additional notes per year, liquidating the value of every outstanding federal reserve note by roughly 10% per annum as a result.

The Progressively owned and controlled corporations, banks and wealthy constituents who had access to this new additional cash when it entered the economy (via the nation's largest banks and brokerage houses) made enormous profits from this added money up front, before it liquidated the value of the remaining money supply. That left the inevitable devaluation to be absorbed by *We the People*—the 99.9%.

This brings us to what is called, The Science of Money, though better named—How to defraud a nation.

The "Science of Money"

The devaluation of our money is nothing more than an insidious tax. As John Maynard Keynes, the Progressive architect of this system of modern counterfeiting by nations (and one of the leading Progressive proponents of fraudulent money) admitted in his 1919 treatise, *The Economic Consequences of the Peace*, that it was to overthrow the existing base of society —a stated goal of Progressivism:

> *"There is no subtler, no surer means of overthrowing the existing base of society than to debauch the currency. The process engages all the hidden forces of economic law on the side of destruction, and does it in a manner which not one man in a million is able to diagnose."*

[Emphasis added]

While sometimes called the "Science of Money" to occlude its real purpose, it is common fraud and it is in violation of the United States Constitution.

The effects of this fraudulent process can be explained as easily as mailing a letter. In my own lifetime of 64 years, a simple government postage stamp has increased from just $.04 to $.50. This represents a 1,250% rate of inflation, or more correctly put, The Federal Reserve has made my dollar worth less than $.08 in six decades. The cost of delivering my letter has not *increased*, in fact, it has gone down significantly; but the value of my *money* has been fraudulently *decreased* to almost nothing.

I've been robbed by a pair of thieves: The (private) Federal Reserve and the Progressives in U.S. government that hired out the printing of counterfeit cash for its own expansion. They stole my dollar and left me 8 cents. Soon, I'll have nothing left. All of my wealth and value will have been transferred by fraud to the .1% who control government and our country today, and I will have paid for the party.

That's the "Science of Money." That's *fiat* currency. That's the Federal Reserve, and that's fraud— the biggest one ever in mankind's history.

Hopefully, the problem created by The Federal Reserve is now clear. Along with the Sixteenth and Seventeenth Amendments, all passed in 1913 at the prompting of the same powerful Progressives who would own the private central bank, our prospects as a free republic became questionable.

The Guardians of Liberty—our State-elected Senators—were illegally re-moved by the Seventeenth Amendment to allow federal government and corporate power to expand without limit or restriction. A private central bank was then created by the Glass-Owen Act, giving the power to print money of no value to the most powerful Progressives in the corporate and banking world: J.P. Morgan, Paul Warburg of the Netherlands and Germany banking family, John D. Rockefeller, and the Rothschild dynasty of England and France.

And the final blow, the Sixteenth Amendment—foisted on us by outright fraud and put into law by their attorney, Secretary of State, Philander C. Knox— gave government the power to tax individual Americans to ensure payment of their enormous fees for making fraudulent money in their private central bank, The Federal Reserve.

As Lord Lionel Walter Rothschild, the son of Nathan Mayer Rothschild, heir to the original Rothschild (Mayer Anselm Bauer), was fond of saying, *"Permit me to issue and control the money of a nation and I care not who makes its laws."*

Once the Rothschild, Morgan, Warburg and Rockefeller coalition controlled America's money through the Federal Reserve, they also did not care who made the laws, as they could control them.

John D. Rockefeller's father-in-law, Senator Nelson Aldrich, ran the Senate Banking Committee, and Rockefeller's New York bank chairman, Benjamin Strong, was put in as the first Chairman of the Federal Reserve. The nation from that day forward belonged to the corporations, just as President Lincoln had feared, foreseen and predicted in his letter to William F. Elkins in 1864.

We Need to Act Now

It is time to take our nation back. The best place to begin that process is by removing control of the nation's money supply from the private central bankers, and returning our country to constitutional money. I believe that Donald J. Trump is the only man since President John Kennedy with the courage to try—and I hope, with a different outcome.

The problem once again is political and educational, as what they have done is illegal. Few Americans have taken the time to understand this process of fake money and its consequences and politicians are also going to be hard to convince that it is time to end their spending orgy—but we're at a point that we must do so or die as a (free) nation.

The means to solve these perplexing problems were provided by three brilliant men over the past quarter century who were kind enough to guide me on this. They include senior Professor of Economics, Walter E. Williams, (George Mason University); Congressman and presidential candidate, Dr. Ron Paul; and central banking historian and constitutionalist, G. Edward Griffin (author of *The Creature from Jekyll Island: A Second Look at the Federal Reserve*). These men graciously took the time in person to discuss these matters with me in interviews over the past 30 years, while I was doing research for this book.

They all three concur that the first step is to repeal all 'legal tender' laws, which require the citizens (under the threat of imprisonment) to use and accept these fraudulent, unconstitutional *Federal Reserve notes*. Professor Williams thoughtfully added the suggestion that all taxes on gold, silver and platinum transactions must also be eliminated to make their use as medium(s) of exchange feasible again. By taxing *real* money, government makes its use impractical and expensive (by intent). Professor Williams reasons this well, *"so there would be no other forms of money, and the government monopoly would be reduced and hence the ability to tax—some would say steal from—us through inflation."*

This would free up the public to innovate other means of exchange during the transition, and put competitive models in place, which would be a good start. Who would want a federal reserve note that is guaranteed to diminish from 1 to .08, when you could have an alternative that stays (at least) at 1 or increases?

Next, the United States Mint was designed to coin the public's gold and silver at little or no cost, in standard weights and measures (a dollar is defined as 371.25 grains of silver in The Coinage Act of 1792, which is still law). Government was not intended to *provide* money, but to produce it from private wealth, guaranteeing only that it was of proper weight and purity.

This needs to be its purpose again. The mint should resume free coinage of the public's gold and silver as currency—or notes backed by it for convenience. Gold must be established as an auxiliary money reserve at free-market value, with only silver at a quantity per dollar. If our society must have a government currency, it needs to be a real one.

We should also be free to create and use other means of exchange like Bitcoin and blockchain innovations, or even private currencies backed by physical commodities of real intrinsic value, like natural resources. Why not real estate, as example—or even stocks? How about an 'Apple dollar' backed by its patents or technology?

There are also successful models of towns and cities using a local currency to encourage shopping in the hometown stores, where all businesses agree to accept the town's dollar. Once freed from the bondage of the Progressive's central bank, the sky is the limit.

But in spite of the Progressives' malicious drowning of our nation in debt, we must honor those obligations. The federal debt should be paid, completely, but we should do so using additional Federal Reserve notes printed solely for that purpose, before its closing. Those obligations were made with the lenders' understanding and expectation that they would be repaid with *Federal Reserve* notes back in 1933, so there would be no fraud in doing so. In order to comply with and honor the Constitution, while putting an end to lawless money, all *Federal Reserve notes*, including the extra and final issue to pay off all federal government debt, must be backed by the nation's reserves of gold and silver.

Another advisor, Ed Griffin, suggested withholding the military's stockpile of gold. I respectfully disagree, if one still exists (See Note at end of chapter) as that would allow our presidents to continue getting the nation in more trouble abroad, if real money were available to them. After the last several administrations' unilaterally declared wars, Mr. Griffin might now agree. All our gold would have been wasted in the Middle East alone.

When Mr. Griffin made his original calculation of the value of a *Federal Reserve note* in his landmark book, *The Creature From Jekyll Island: A Second Look at The Federal Reserve*, it was based on 1993 figures. One *Federal Reserve note* was equal to .0047 silver dollar, or differently stated, it took 213 *Federal Reserve notes* to make one real or *constitutional* dollar.

The U.S. Debt Clock showed the United States Debt as $21,175,819,252,324 on May 6th, 2018 at 1:45 p.m. Central European Time, and was growing so fast I had to pick which last four digits to use (`http: //www.usdebtclock.org/`).

The U. S. government's gold supply is estimated at 260 million ounces according to an article I found in Forbes Magazine by Todd Ganos, which I had to rely on as no public information is available. (`www.forbes. com/sites/toddganos/2013/07/07/is-gold-really-worth-40000-per- ounce/\#47ca4a157ea8`)

While gold is not the standard under our law, silver is, gold is a real store of value. Silver stores have been depleted or coined (see Note at end of chapter) but we will use the 1993 level to be conservative in our estimates. Gold presently sells at 80 times the price of silver ($16.52/ ounce), so that will be its valuation for this calculation. Inventories of U.S. gold and silver generously become valued at:

Silver - 320,000,000 ounces @ $16.52/oz	$ 5,286,400,000
Gold - 260,000,000 ounces @ 80 x 16.52	$343,616,000,000
Market value today	$348,902,400,000
Debt (05/06/2018)	$21,175,819,252,324
Outstanding currency	$ 41,600,000,000
Total	$21,217,419,252,324

That is a ratio of 60.8:1 in debt to the constitutional monetary value held by the United States today.

If the estimated $54 trillion in unfunded payments to the American people for Social Security, Medicare and Medicaid are included, then that ratio becomes 215:1.

Would you keep loaning money to someone who had $215.58 dollars of debt already, against every $1 in assets? Not likely, and this fact has occurred to the foreign nations who once bought our debt as well. They have stopped. So guess what they're doing now?

This is How Bad it has Gotten Under the Progressives

The Federal Reserve is now 'buying' U.S. Treasury bills to create the debt instruments, and then printing money against that debt to fund government overspending that foreign nations are reluctant to fund any more. This is incestuous, dangerous, and unsustainable. And it has to stop.

Once the final printing of *Federal Reserve notes* necessary to cover all existing federal debt is completed, a debt-free nation must move forward, spending only its revenue derived from legal, constitutional taxes and sources. By limiting its funds, this should force Congress to live by Article I, Section 8 as well as the Tenth Amendment which precludes them from any activity not listed therein. That could put an end to overreach into areas where federal government has no legal authority.

Once backed by the nation's gold and silver stores, the trillions of *Federal Reserve notes* in circulation around the world will have a real value and can be used as money until they are retired, but the American people can no longer be *forced* to use this unlawful money at the point of a gun as is the case today.

Government will have to accept the *Federal Reserve notes* it authorized as payment for its taxes or any other public obligation— just as it will do to foreign nations—and they can be used with other members of the public as long as the other party is *willing* to accept them. Real money, privately or publicly produced, however, would also be available for commerce, ending the harmful boom-bust cycles and constant erosion of value inherent with the *fiat* money of no real value manufactured by The Federal Reserve of today.

The Federal Reserve System itself could then become nothing more than a private check-clearing service for banks, without any monetary authority, and no further power to lower the value of our money. As John Stuart Mill wrote in 1848 of debt issuers, they...

> *"may have, and in the case of a government paper always have, a direct interest in lowering the value of the currency because it is the medium in which their own debts are computed."*

This debauchery is theft, and the time to end it is now, while we have someone in the White House with the courage to do so.

Action Plan

We must begin by repealing the Federal Reserve Act (Glass-Owen) and all "legal tender" laws requiring the use or acceptance of federal reserve notes, except that government must accept them for taxes and payments. As soon as the final printing or electronic creation of all Federal Reserve Notes needed to pay all debts and legal obligations of the federal government has been completed, its authority and control ends.

Taxes on gold, silver and platinum transactions must be abolished, so they may be used as money without additional transaction costs or fees.

The United States Mint should be reopened for free coinage of the public's gold and silver, basing the value of a "dollar" at 371.25 grains of silver (.7734375 troy ounces), as required to be the standard under the United States Constitution and law.

By establishing gold as an auxiliary money reserve at free-market value, coined at specific weights (but not denominated in value) it can float against the silver "standard" dollar—and the federal government can agree to hold private gold and issue official United States dollars against it. That's constitutional money—backed by something real rather than just debt.

All federal holdings of gold and silver not held for others to print real U.S. dollars, must be used to back the *Federal Reserve notes* issued and outstanding to make them constitutionally legal money for continued use until retired, while allowing no more to be created.

The world will scream bloody murder when their share of America's debt is repaid at pennies on the dollar, but they agreed to be repaid in worthless federal reserve notes, and what they are getting instead, even with minimal backing, is actually worth *something*, which the federal reserve note was not. They will get over it, eventually, and we will be debt free.

Starting now, however, while the President sells this idea of returning to real money to Congress and the American people, we should immediately start allowing the public to create its own means of exchanges, including barter, product and service exchanges, private and/or electronic digital currencies, block-chain currencies such as Bitcoin, and any other means they choose as a free people. Many alternatives will certainly make the transition easier, and there is only the imagination to limit what amazing ideas come forth.

Note: According to the Silver Users Association, the United States store of this metal may already have been liquidated: *"In the early 1980's, the U.S. government's strategic stockpile of silver was locked in by law at 139.5 Million oz. Congress has since authorized legislation to dispose of these stockpiles. In late 2000 the U.S. Defense National Stockpile Center delivered its remaining stockpile of nearly 15 Million oz. to the U.S. Mint for coinage programs. Since 2001, the U.S. has had to purchase silver for its coinage programs from the open market. This has boosted silver consumption by 1% annually."* Source: (`http://www.silverusersassociation.org/silver/uspolicies.shtml`)

Chapter 7

PUT PANDORA BACK IN HER BOX

ARGUMENTS having been made for what got our nation in trouble (and suggestions made for how to extricate ourselves), it is proper now to discuss what federal government is *supposed* to do for *We the People.*

What are its legitimate duties? What, if any, are its limits?

The answer to the first question, "What are its legitimate duties?," can be summed up in two words, "very few." The federal government is extremely limited in its (lawful) duties and powers, each specifically listed in Article I, Section 8 of the United States Constitution.

"What are its limits?" They are stringent and exact. Anything not specifically listed in the Constitution as a duty or power of federal government, is forbidden. Unless positively stated as its function in the Constitution, the Tenth Amendment of the Bill or Rights precludes federal government from it. James Madison's words were clear:

"The powers not delegated to the United States by the Constitution, nor prohibited by it to the States, are reserved to the States respectively, or to the people." AMENDMENT X, UNITED STATES CONSTITUTION

What Can Federal Government Legally Do?

By turning to Appendix A, the actual duties can be seen and read as James Madison wrote them. They are few and limited. In essence, they allow federal government to raise money for its own operation, through specified means; they are authorised to organize a navy to provide for the common defense; and to carry out duties which would be expected at the union level, such as postal service, courts for disputes between citizens and governments of different States or nations, establish treaties, and develop a common set of standard weights and measures. (See Article I, Section 8 in Appendix A)

If needed for defense, and only then, an army could be raised for no more than two years by calling up the State militias. That is only if Congress voted to declare war, which has not happened since World War II.

Federal government can regulate interstate commerce to keep it open and free, set up a patent office, and punish crimes external to the United States such as *"Piracies and Felonies committed on the high Seas, and Offenses against the Laws of Nations"*. It can also *"provide for the Punishment of counterfeiting the Securities and current Coin of the United States,"* to protect the integrity of money and government securities.

That is all. The alphabet soup of federal bureaucracies such as the DOJ (Department of Justice), FBI, NSA, EPA, FDA, HUD, DOE, NRO, NIH, CDC, FEMA, DEA, ATF, DHS, plus sixteen spy agencies, our standing army—the largest in the world—and all the rest whose powers are not specifically granted in Article I, Section 8, are *unconstitutional*. I suggest that you take a few minutes and read the Constitution for yourself. It is not that long and its words are so clear and simple that a child could understand what it says and means. As I say often, *"It takes a lawyer to misinterpret the Constitution and nine of them in black robes to completely ignore it."* After you've read it for yourself, you will understand that as well.

None of the alphabet agencies listed above or their powers are listed as duties of federal government and are therefore precluded by the Tenth Amendment, so every person working in them is doing so in violation of their oath of office to uphold the Constitution. Perhaps President Trump —should he be bold enough to terminate the lower tier for such 'cause'— could offer them immunity from prosecution under 18 U.S.C. §§241, 242, if they voluntary resign with a transition stipend, and agree to cooperate with investigators regarding the heads of their agencies. The Comeys, Clappers, Rosensteins, McCabes, Lerners, Lynches, Brennans, Strzoks, Pages, Ohrs, Muellers, and so on are what 'Andy' (Andrew Weissman) would call *kingpins* and no deals should be made, just give them a "*Speedy and Public Trial*" as required under the Sixth Amendment—something none of them ever did for us—and hang them.

While joking a bit on some of this—(except the part about hanging Comey, Clapper, Mueller and Rosenstein, and of course 'Andy' ;-))— I believe that some form of deal with teeth in it is possible and should be done to eliminate these unconstitutional departments.

The Deep State would be gone, the duties performed by those agencies that are truly needed would be transferred to the States (or eliminated) and since those millions of people will be looking for real employment, they'll vote for Donald Trump in spite of hating him, as they know there is no hope for new jobs for them if the the Pelosi/Schumer/ Sanders Soros/Bezos-backed "Progressive" Socialists ever get back in.

And there is not a one of these agencies or people we would not be better off without in reality. Not one. Even if one of them were of any positive value, their very existence is unlawful. Those duties belong to the States and people, not federal government—and perhaps those who accept voluntary dismissal without reprisal could be first in line for those positions across the heartland.

And as for the 16 illegal spy agencies and the domestic snoops at the NSA, if we need to spy on other nations, Naval Intelligence can legally do it, but they are the only ones. If politicians want to spy on us, then they should hire a private investigator using their own money, as doing so through their "National Security Agency" is not an allowed duty of government and therefore, forbidden.

The best description of the separation and limitations between federal and State powers can again be found in the words of the Constitution's main author, James Madison:

> *"The powers delegated by the proposed Constitution to the federal government are few and defined. Those which are to remain in the State governments are numerous and indefinite. The former will be exercised principally on external objects, [such] as war, peace, negotiations, and foreign commerce....The powers reserved to the several States will extend to objects which, in the ordinary course of affairs, concern the lives, liberties, and properties of the people."*
>
> The Federalist #45

There can be no question as to the Founders' intent when the author of the Constitution stated it so clearly. Federal government was to be lean, efficient and kept out of the nation's internal affairs. It was to be as removed as possible from the daily lives of the citizens. The critical areas of day-to-day governance were held to be the province of the States— or left alone—our first right as citizens. Federal government was then precluded from exceeding these strict boundaries by the *'Constitution'* and is clearly in violation of it today. In fact, almost nothing it does has root in the Constitution and this must change.

The preponderance of power was, by contract, to remain with the sovereign States and people. Federal government was to deal with externals such as defense from attack; while the States retained authority over internal matters that affected the people.

Since Progressives set loose the Three Horsemen of the Apocalypse in 1913, Congress has inserted itself into every nook and cranny of the private lives of its citizens, though contracted to leave us alone and protect us from such tyranny of others.

From the moment the federally-controlled radio station on the alarm clock comes alive as the morning wake-up call, through the morning cup of federally-taxed coffee and the drive to work on federal highways paid for by federal gasoline taxes; until the end of the day, where over half of the average American's daily wages will be robbed in some other form of tax, the federal government has wormed and intertwined itself into the lives of its citizens' every move, moment and dollar.

Under so-called 'progressivism' the federal government of the United States of America has become that against which it fought for most of our nation's history.

How Bad is It?

As the comic strip character in *Pogo* once said, "*I have seen the enemy and it is us.*" The once-revered *land of the free* cannot stay atop its own index created to judge others, as briefly referenced. The vaunted Freedom House, was founded in 1941 by Americans concerned with the advance of fascism, but it reluctantly dropped its own founding nation to Forty-third place, well behind many of those it once criticized and vilified for the same practices now employed by the United States (Annual Report-2007). The Freedom House was absorbed by Progressive groups during the Obama years and no longer reports.

But before becoming a Progressive tool, the attendant report from 2007, "*Today's America: How Free?*", cited abuses for which the United States had become known under both President Bush and Obama, such as its secret torture camps around the world, "extraordinary rendition" (illegal kidnapping), broad and uncontrolled wiretapping by the NSA and other federal entities, and the rise in the number of documents classified and kept from *We the People*, which the study states, *"has jumped from 8.7m in 2001 to 14.2m in 2005....a 60% increase over 3 years."*

The study excoriated the criminal justice system which has replaced America's once-respected and admired federal judiciary. It has become little more than a conviction machine for the 314,000+ federal statutes with prison as a penalty. The study cites the explosion of the number of citizens in American gulags from *"1.39 per 1,000 in 1980 to 7.5 in 2006."*

But as our freedoms continued to erode under the Bush Administration through the Obama years, the ranking simply disappeared. Freedom House is now a Progressive front, supporting Progressive protest groups seeking to reduce freedoms, rather than ranking nations by the ones they actually have left. If you can't beat 'em, buy 'em.

The true number of American prisoners was first exposed by then-Senator Jim Webb (D-VA) in March of 2009. In a national article in Parade Magazine, Webb disclosed the nation's secret:

> *"1 in 31 Americans are in the corrections system today. Either we are the most evil people on earth or we are doing something very wrong."*

America's penal colonies and corrections system according to Senator Webb actually held 7.3 million—a record for human history. To put this in perspective, Communist China incarcerates only one of every 1,272 of its citizens, meaning an American citizen is over thirty-six times more likely to be in this nation's corrections system than a communist Chinese citizen. If that does not get your attention, I don't know what will.

As can readily be seen in Article 1, Section 8, most of the statutes fabricated by Congress to send Americans to prison, exceed federal constitutional authority. Federal government does not have legal jurisdiction to do this—yet it does it every day—and 'Andy' and the schlock on the bench send them away for years and decades, never blinking or questioning what they are doing or how they can justify it under the Constitution they swore to uphold.

Our so-called leaders have turned the nation into the very definition of a police state. There are currently over 18,000 separate police agencies operating within our borders. Though many nations are far more populous than the United States, no tyrant or dictator has ever had such an astounding number.

As the Pogo character said once again, "*We have seen the enemy,*" and I'll add "*it is our own representatives in Congress who have done this to us.*" They should be imprisoned for such senseless violations of our Constitution and freedoms. There is no excuse for what Congress has done and allowed.

Congress had no power to create but a handful of laws, and no authority to create the vast majority of federal agencies which police them any more than the Executive Branch had the power to create its Department of Justice, its NSA, its FBI, or its 16 spy agencies, as will be discussed in the next chapter.

Is Change In The Wind?

Many of the States' legislatures are finally beginning to listen to their citizens and wake up. *We the People* had enough long ago. In the relatively moderate State of Oklahoma, as example, House Joint Resolution 1089, sponsored by Representative Charles Key, passed by an overwhelming 92 to 3 in 2008. It put the federal servant-cum-master on notice.

The resolution stated:

> *"Whereas the Tenth Amendment defines the total scope of federal power as being that specifically granted by the Constitution of the United States and no more; and whereas, the scope of power defined by the Tenth Amendment means that the federal government was created by the states specifically to be an agent of the states; and whereas, today in 2008, the states are demonstrably treated as agents of the federal government..... Now, therefore, be it resolved by the House of Representatives and the Senate of the 2nd session of the 51ˢᵗ Oklahoma Legislature: that the State of Oklahoma hereby claims sovereignty under the Tenth Amendment to the Constitution of the United States over all powers not otherwise enumerated and granted to the federal government by the Constitution of the United States. This serves as Notice and Demand to the federal government, as our agent, to cease and desist, effective immediately, mandates that are beyond the scope of these constitutionally delegated powers."*

Such action by Representative Key and the Oklahoma House of Representatives is a template for all other sovereign States. The Oklahoma Senate did not have the courage to follow through on the resolution (and was pressured by the federal government to go into recess to avoid it) but public anger over federal government's destruction of the nation and our liberties will force them to act at some point, or such cowardly senators will lose their seats.

The State of California will vote on a proposal to secede from the Union in the fall of 2018, and during the Obama years, *thirty state governments* were served secession petitions by the required number of their citizens to force it to be considered. Thirty out of fifty!

Do I want this movement to succeed or see my nation torn apart between Americans and those who would change what that means? Of course not, and by returning to constitutional government (and expelling those from government who swore to uphold the Constitution, but have instead thwarted it) we no longer have a crisis. But such hardline disfavor with the results of a century of Progressivism by 30 of the 50 United States is a very real indicator of how far our federal government has exceeded its mandate.

Once again, it is time for a Convention of States to resolve these matters, but in the interim, every state following the example of Oklahoma Resolution 1089 would put Congress on notice to get its head out of the sand or we will do it for them.

Action Plan

Pressure your state'a legislators to introduce and pass resolutions like Senator Charles Key's in Oklahoma, putting federal government on notice of its breach of contract. Order it to cease and desist in its unlawful activities.

Organize grassroots campaign to elect only Representatives to federal government who will vote to nullify the 300,000+ statutes illegally made into law by "Administrative process" instead of Congress and signed by a president—and make *that* a crime.

Further, any of the 14,000+ laws which are not under federal government's purview as defined in Article I, Section 8, but were passed unlawfully by Congress to be used by 'Andy' to imprison us are prohibited by the Tenth Amendment from being under federal purview and authority. They've got to go as well.

Also, we need to get back to a better class of judges who support law and Constitution instead of ignoring it, which means we should support and elect candidates for the U.S. Senate who pledge to recommend only candidates for federal judgeships, including the Supreme Court who:

1. Have never been a prosecutor, and;

2. Will pledge to dismiss any criminal charges or convictions under laws which are not rightfully the purview of federal government, as is their responsibility under law and Constitution.

Support only candidates for Congress who will pledge to eliminate agencies of federal government not specifically authorized by the U.S. Constitution to speed an end to federal control of our lives. The Tenth Amendment precludes the national government from such involvement. That is the law.

We can once again take a much faster step by supporting the call for a Convention of States to bring federal government back to Constitutional and Rule of Law and limits.

Notes From History That Should Guide Us

"The general rule is that an unconstitutional statute, though having the form and name of law, is in reality no law, but is wholly void, and ineffective for any purpose; since unconstitutionality dates from the time of its enactment, and not merely from the date of the decision so branding it. No one is bound to obey an unconstitutional law and no courts are bound to enforce it."

16 Am Jur 2d. §177. late 2d. §256

"An unconstitutional act is not law; it confers no rights; it imposes no duties; affords no protection; it creates no office; it is in legal contemplation, as inoperative as though it had never been passed."

Norton v. Shelby County, 118 US 425, 30 L Ed 178, 6 S.Ct. 1121 (1886)

"Where rights secured by the Constitution are involved, there can be no rule making or legislation which would abrogate them.", Miranda v. Arizona. 384 US 436, 16 L Ed 2d 120, 105 S. Ct. 1602 (1966)

"All laws which are repugnant to the Constitution are null and void."

Marbury v. Madison, 5 US 137,2 L Ed 60 (1803)

Stare decisis (case law) is held sacrosanct by our courts today, while such sensible decisions as above are completely ignored. Instead, Progressively invented "Administrative laws" are implemented and enforced outside of law and Constitution.

That is why I suggest that we must return to choosing judges who are not former prosecutors or even lawyers (as was allowed up until the 1970s in my home state of North Carolina) but rather solid citizens who can read the simple words of James Madison (the non-lawyer who is credited as being the principle author of the U.S. Constitution).

Chapter 8

THE MOST POWERFUL MAN IN THE WORLD?

THE position of President and Chief Executive of the United States, under the constitutional confines of Article II at any rate, is a rather mundane job except perhaps during time of war.

A *constitutional* president has very little power rather than being "the most powerful in the world," as many say today. He or she is allowed to sign legislation written and approved by others—not create it. The president has the power of appointments to certain posts, and is titular head and Commander of the nation's defense forces, but only when an actual war has been officially declared by Congress—another branch of government.

Article II, Section 2, is clear about the only time this duty is held: "*The President shall be Commander in Chief of the Army and Navy of the United States, and the Militia of the several States, when called into actual Service of the United States.*" [Emphasis added] Only Congress can do that, and absent a declaration of war, starting a war is a violation of law and the president has no legal authority over the military.

It is Congress's job "*To declare War*", "*To raise and support Armies,*" "*To provide and maintain a Navy*", and "*To provide for calling forth the Militia*".

(Article I, Section 8, U.S. Constitution) It is even the job of Congress *"To provide for organizing, arming, and disciplining, the Militia, and for governing such Part of them as may be employed in the Service of the United States."* (Ibid) So even as Commander in Chief, there is little for a *constitutional* president to do. Congress has the responsibility for most of the heavy lifting.

The president can also *"make Treaties"* but only *"with the Advice and consent of the Senate... provided two thirds of the Senators present concur."* (Article II, Section 2, U.S. Constitution)

The president can *"receive Ambassadors and other Public Ministers"*, *"take Care that the Laws be faithfully executed"*, and *"shall Commission all the Officers of the United States."* The only other constitutional duty he has is to *"grant Reprieves and Pardons for Offenses against the United States, except in cases of Impeachment."* (Article II, Section 2, U.S. Constitution)

That's it, folks. The president is our nation's host or hostess, and the last stop for a piece of legislation.

A *constitutional* president is clearly one with plenty of time on his hands, who has almost no effect on the lives of the people of the nation, nor was he or she supposed to.

So What Happened?

The President was intended to be a figurehead and little else. Any other powers outside of these listed are forbidden to the President by the Tenth Amendment of the U.S. Constitution. This is the law. This is how it is supposed to be, but this is not how it is today in post-constitutional America. The Progressives turned this humble post once peopled by (mostly) humble men into an imperial one with unlimited power—as long as he or she was in the Progressive's own ranks or brought to power by them and their money.

An enemy of their elite kingdom—such as President Donald Trump—will be attacked using every legal and illegal means at their disposal, even from within the palace itself, to take down a usurper of what they consider *their* power. Constitution be damned.

Of course, the Constitution has been damned for one hundred years under their almost exclusive rule, or the presidency would never have been endowed with such duties and powers never imagined by the Founders or in their constitution, and in most cases, in direct opposition to it.

From the constitutional role as a somewhat insignificant figurehead of a severely limited federal government, the office of President of the United States has been illegitimately expanded to the most powerful position in the world. Its misdeeds and abuses have the potential to affect every life on earth, and to even end life on earth as we know it.

Aside from being completely outside of our nation's own laws and government's legitimate limits, it is dangerous to the world to have one man or woman, a politician at that, with such power over mankind as a whole.

The office of the presidency and the powers usurped by the Progressives holding that office, have become far too powerful and it is in contractual breach with the People who granted government and president their powers in the first place.

While I firmly believe that there is finally a president in power who is simply there to do the right thing rather than to just *be in power,* that also makes him the one who might actually try to reduce the power of that office to prevent further abuses by his successors.

So Let's Do Inventory

From this limited base of legal duties described above, the presidency now manages sixteen unconstitutional spy agencies, has direct responsibility for a national police force (FBI) which has been used for the last twenty years to rough up those deemed out of step with the Progressive ideology. He is over an internal spy agency to monitor and snoop on domestic enemies of Progressivism (National Security Agency), and presidents starting with Abraham Lincoln gave themselves the power to legislate from the White House using an unconstitutional tool with no basis in law known as an Executive Order.

To be clear, an order from the Office of the Executive to one of the departments under his purview, is legal. An Executive Order, however, which is treated as having force of law, is not. There is a huge difference that has been intentionally blurred. One is doing his job, the other is legislating from the White House, which is a no-no.

Presidents now start unilateral wars (e.g. Kennedy-Cuba, Reagan-Grenada, Bush I-Panama, Clinton-Bosnia, Serbia, Haiti; Bush II-Iraq and Afghanistan; Obama-Somalia and Pakistan). They break treaties instead of making them, debase the currency instead of protecting it, sanction the murder of "*Ambassadors and other Public Ministers*" rather than just "*receiving*" them, and oversee the most powerful standing army in the world during times of undeclared war, none of which is legal or constitutional.

The abuse which feeds the misdeeds of the presidency more than any other, in my opinion, is the unconstitutional *executive order*. That is a power not found in Article II and is therefore forbidden. It is a means of by-passing Congress and usurping its powers, but as the presidency has also become the titular head of a political party (another anomaly not anticipated by the Founding Fathers) it becomes less and less likely that Congress will challenge expanded presidential authorities unless a non-Progressive somehow runs the gauntlet and gets in like Donald Trump —against all odds.

Congress's own activities and legislation can rarely find root in Section 8 of Article I, as is required by the Constitution as well, so they are in poor position to challenge unconstitutional Executive authority or Judicial misconduct. All three branches are fouled and saying anything about the other would be the pot calling the kettle black for sure.

The Supreme Court, as discussed, has been scared of its own shadow since Chief Justice Hughes caved in to President Franklin D. Roosevelt in 1937, and has shown no stomach for challenging either branch— or preserving the Founders' instituted restraints, as is their mission and sole purpose for being.

So Where Are We?

We are now left without the amazing system of checks and balances designed, and have only wilful blindness by each branch of government to the other branches' illegitimate behavior—perhaps out of fear of being challenged on their own—and the balance between State and Federal powers has been all but obliterated and sucked to the Foggy Bottom Swamp.

The first of these unconstitutional *executive orders* or proclamations was issued by Abraham Lincoln in 1861 at the outbreak of the War Between the States. Executive Order #1 suspended the writ of *habeas corpus*, which is the most basic protection of individual liberty. This is the right to be brought before the court to challenge illegal detention. (Article I, Section 9, U.S. Constitution)

"The presidential act was challenged by Chief Justice Roger Taney who, in the case of Ex parte Merryman, vigorously contended that the power of suspension resided only in Congress. Lincoln ignored the order of the court".[1] Lincoln set two precedents still carried on to this day—1) using an illegal device known as an executive order—and 2) ignoring the law, as have 100 years of presidents since and including Wilson, and doing what they want.

---

[1] Encyclopaedia Brittanica, Vol. 5, Micropaedia, p. 601

Some of the most dangerous seeds of the nation and world's potential destruction have been sown by U.S. presidents using this power which they don't have under law or their contract with *We the People*. The power to make laws resides with Congress alone.

President Theodore Roosevelt next used this illegitimate tool to establish his federal bureau of investigation (FBI). In 1907, he asked Congress to create it, but was rebuffed. Roosevelt was correctly informed by Senator Benjamin "Pitchfork" Tillman that there was no such authorization in the Constitution for a national police force. That was not (and is not) an allowed duty of the federal government.

Undaunted by constitution, law, or Congress, President Roosevelt created his *federal bureau of investigation* outside of law, using the fraud Lincoln once employed to suspend the constitutional privilege of *habeas corpus*—an *executive order*.

By 1908, Roosevelt had his illegal operation up and running and put it under the purview of his attorney general, Charles J. Bonaparte, descendant of French Emperor, Napoleon Bonaparte. The new agents were soon caught going through the mail of Senator Benjamin Ryan "Pitchfork" Tillman,[2] who had refused to legislate such an illegal government force and he and Roosevelt *"became such bitter enemies that at one point the President barred Tillman from the White House."*[3]

Fast Forward to Today

Roosevelt's FBI was unconstitutional then, it is unconstitutional now, has never been authorized by Congress, and it is still snooping through private citizens' mail (and worse) a century later. It was only learned in

---

[2]Walker, Samuel. Popular Justice: A History of American Criminal Justice,2nd Ed. (1997) Oxford Univ. Press, p. 139

[3]Encyclopaedia Brittanica, Vol.11, Micropaedia, p. 776

May of 2018, that the Progressive cabal running the CIA, FBI, and other of these unconstitutional agencies—assisted by the State Department— actually planted spies within the campaign of then-candidate, Donald Trump, intended to insure that their candidate, Hillary Clinton, won. They then added their now infamous "insurance policy," according to co-conspirators, Sztrok and Page, (in one of the 'Andy's' offices) in the unlikely event that their stacked deck did not succeed during the election, so they could take the president down afterwards.

CIA Chief, John Brennan, actually made a trip to Russia to consort with Russian operatives on the plan, and the State Department co-ordinated with the FBI and CIA to allow a visa to be issued to State-Department banned Russian attorney, Natalia Veselnitskaya, to help them set up the Trump campaign for a later attempt by these same people to make it appear that Trump had "colluded" with the Russians—though the Progressive cabal members conspiring to do these unlawful acts actually did collude with Russian operatives to set him up—a factoid lost on the Progressive media!

An intentionally *salacious and unverified* dossier, to quote James Comey, former FBI Director who aided and abetted in this criminal conduct, was later publicly discredited, but it was put together by spooks at home and abroad for *Progressive* spooks at home breaking the law and was paid for by the Clinton campaign and Democratic National Committee, who believed beyond all doubt that she would win and their criminal conduct would never be found out.

That was actually a reasonable assumption because every single member of upper management at all of these agencies were unabashed Progressives who would profit in terms of power when their girl won. Who could unseat them or claim they had done wrong? They controlled the entire power structure of prosecution, conviction and punishment! They were above the law, 'cause no one could go after them but themselves— which clearly needs to change, and I have an idea for that.

The same Progressive cabal now trying to take down President Trump—Rod Rosenstein, James Comey, John Brennan, Andrew McCabe, Andrew Weissman, et al, —used this knowingly false 'dossier' paid for by Mrs. Clinton and the DNC to illegally get FISA court warrants to spy on her opponent, Donald J. Trump, his family, and his campaign.

This is criminal conduct of the highest order, in a blatant attempt by Progressive candidates *cum* losers to bring down a duly elected president in an unlawfully cobbled together *coup d'etat*.

How Did We Get Here?

There is no doubt that Progressive Theodore Roosevelt started the Executive Branch down this slippery slope by starting an Executive Branch detective service to perform takedowns of political adversaries. The next Progressive Roosevelt who became president, Franklin Delano, followed Teddy's suit by creating the equally unlawful OSS (Office of Strategic Services) in June of 1942, to coordinate the intelligence gathering functions of the army and navy, under William J.("Wild Bill") Donovan.[4]

The OSS was dismantled at the end of World War II in October of 1945, but government had tasted the forbidden fruit of unsupervised spying and wanted more of it.

When Harry S. Truman succeeded Roosevelt as president, he "*established by executive order a Central Intelligence Group and a National Intelligence Authority. The bodies selected key personnel from the motley group assembled under wartime pressures by the OSS and tried to impose some central direction on postwar intelligence operations, although the armed forces maintained their independent intelligence services.*"[5] [Emphasis added]

---

[4]Ibid., Vol. 3, p.28, Central Intelligence Agency
[5]Ibid.

The 'Motley Group' at Work

This "motley group" as the Encyclopaedia Brittanica kindly describes these remnant rogues, reported directly to the Executive Branch, which illegally created these organizations outside of constitutional authority using means not found in law. The CIA has been responsible for wars, murder, and mayhem ever since, in the name of whomever was president at that time and usually in support of whoever were the then-president's largest donors ranging from United Fruit when they began to Halliburton today.

The encyclopedia credits the CIA with such international terrorist acts as *"the expulsion of Mohammad Mossaddeq as premier"* [of Iran] in 1953, *"the toppling of an unfriendly leftist government in Guatemala,"* in 1954, and *"the attempted Bay of Pigs invasion of Cuba,"* in 1961. The encyclopedia also briefly mentions the revelation that *"former CIA operatives had reputedly played illegal roles in the Watergate affair."*[6]

The Brittanica Encyclopaedia was chosen as the source for much of this, as the information itself has the potential to be inflammatory, and is far less kindly handled by other sources.

What the encyclopedia fails to share with its readers is the fact that the legitimate leader of Iran, Mohammed Mossadegh, whom the CIA deposed under Kermit Roosevelt's direction (President Theodore Roosevelt's grandson), was Time Magazine's *Man of the Year* in 1954. He was responsible for taking back control of his nation's oil resources from British Petroleum, which had stolen them by force of arms under the British Army. His crime was taking back resources stolen from his nation by a foreign power for a private corporation, at the end of a gun—a now familiar storyline that should make my point.

---

[6] Ibid.

The CIA's Guatemalan escapade referenced by the encyclopedia was its overthrow of democratically elected President Jacobo Arbenz so he could be replaced by dictator Colonel Carlos Castillo Armas to do the CIA's (and United Fruit's) bidding. Each of these acts is terrorism by the definition of the term stated by United Nations Secretary General, Kofi Annan, after the 9/11 attack in New York in 2001.

Recent books revealing these misdeeds are chronicled and supported in M.I.T. Professor Noam Chomsky's tome, *Failed States*, and by former company insider John Perkins in *The Secret History of the American Empire*. These two well-known and reliable authors detailed from public records (or personal knowledge, in the case of Perkins) that the executive branch and its CIA have participated in untold murders, overthrows, terrorist actions and coups—the most recent being the one now going on in the United States against President Donald J. Trump.

Obama's CIA director, John Brennan, himself has been found to be a part of the coup attempt, as well as lying to Congress under oath, but nothing has been done about this to date, and 'Andy' is unlikely to do so, which has become a practice so standard—refusal to equally enforce the law—that we must do something about it, including perhaps, shutting them down completely until someone can find a "Department of Justice" mentioned or authorized in the Constitution. (Trust me, they can't).

What can we do about it? We can follow the lead of other nations that have faced this same problem successfully. The United States is the only remaining nation claiming to be free or democratic that has not established Offices of Federal Ombudsman to deal with bad actors within the government itself. These courts could be established by Congress as Article III courts, specifically empowered to charge, prosecute and sentence those within government who violate the rights of citizens, but are presently above the law by their own.

This would include every federal judge and prosecutor who knowingly or intentionally violates the constitutional rights of those brought before them, and every politician or employee who violates their oath of office, as there is no (working) mechanism at present to bring these people to justice.

This is not a new idea or my own, but a tried and true means of bringing transparency to government and holdings its bad actors accountable. Sweden was the first nation to set up offices of federal ombudsmen, followed by Norway, Finland, and Denmark—now ranked as the four most transparent governments in the world.

This office would also be able to question illegal government practices abroad, which brings us back to the rogue agencies and what they have done in the past.

A list of the various terrorist acts committed by our spy forces gleaned from just these two authors (Perkins and Chomsky) include the attempted overthrow in 1963 of Abdul Karim Qasim by CIA operative, Saddam Hussein. Saddam failed, so the CIA executed Qasim on TV by firing squad, much like its hanging of Saddam himself 40 years later. The CIA then sponsored the killing of 5,000 innocents.

Other incidents reported and confirmed by Perkins and Chomsky include the 1964 overthrow of Victor Paz Estenssoro, president of Bolivia, Three years later, CIA agent Felix Rodriguez illegally entered the country and murdered Argentine Che Guevara in La Higuera, Bolivia. Salvador Allende was overthrown by the CIA in Chile (1973), just as they had over thrown President João Belchior Marques Goulart of Brazil a decade earlier. President Jaime Roldos of Ecuador was assassinated in a CIA-coordinated plane crash in 1981, as was Omar Torrijos of Panama, that same year.

More recently, President Hugo Chavez dodged two CIA/Executive Branch attempted murders and an overthrow. The bitter backlash from these acts of terrorism have fueled the animus now seen against the United States by these same nations and should be no surprise—but there was no means of bringing the people who committed or authorized the acts of terror to justice.

Murdering and over-throwing duly elected heads of states to take control of their natural resources or to install a puppet dictator not of that people's choosing, are not things quickly or easily forgotten, any more than Americans will easily forget the attack on New York by Saudi Arabians on September 11, 2001.[7] The bitter fruits of America's own terrorist activities have come home to roost.

International crimes by these rogue agencies have not been limited to South and Central America alone. In 1963, President Kennedy ordered the assassination of our ally, South Vietnamese President Ngo Dinh Diem. Recently, Ken Saro Wiwa and 8 other environmentalists were hanged under Executive/CIA pressure for standing up to Shell Oil (and the CIA) in Nigeria. CIA sponsored terrorist activities have taken the United States from the most respected and trusted nation on earth, to last place, tied with its one-time arch-enemy, Russia, as the least-trusted and most dangerous, in a study cited by Noam Chomsky in *Failed States*.[8]

France and Communist China have taken the nation's place as most respected and trusted, in recent international polls. Even Mexico, our closest neighbor, sees the United States as *'the most dangerous nation on the planet,'* according to polls cited by Chomsky.

The man who coordinated much of this terrorist activity for presidents over recent years, from Chomsky's research, was John Negroponte. Negroponte ran covert operations and terrorist training camps out of Honduras under the Reagan administration. President George W. Bush made this man Deputy Secretary of State under Condoleeza Rice, who

---

[7] "The **hijackers in the** September11attacks were 19 men affiliated with al-Qaeda. Fifteen of the 19 were citizens of SaudiArabia, and the others were from the UnitedArabEmirates (2), Egypt, and Lebanon." One might ask why America invaded oil-rich Iraq and heroin-rich Afghanistan in retaliation for what mostly Saudis terrorist did, though I think by now you can figure it out. (Source of quote, Wikipedia). These invasions by U.S. troops were certainly not about 'weapons of mass destruction.'

[8] *Chomsky, p. 28*

was seriously considered as a draft choice as the Republican candidate to face Barack Obama in 2008. The United States was only a nomination away from having a man considered by many nations as the Western world's equivalent of Osama bin Laden, elevated to being America's representative to the other nations of the globe as Secretary of State.

Prior to his appointment as Deputy Secretary, Negroponte headed and coordinated the activities of all sixteen of the executive branch's unconstitutional spy agencies, not one of which has ever been authorized by Congress. They were created by *executive order*, because they were illegal and Congress knew it.

Perhaps the most insidious and unquestionably, the largest of these shadowy organizations is the NSA (National Security Agency) which was created outside of constitution and law in 1952 by President Harry S. Truman, again, using an *executive order*.[9]

Even the most flattering and mundane description of this agency, whose principle activity is spying on the American people, infers its illegality, as now confirmed by Eric Snowden, the NSA whistleblower.

As for the domestic spy operation the Encyclopedia Brittanica entry states: "*The NSA grew out of the communications intelligence activities of U.S. military units during World War II. The NSA was established in 1952 by a presidential directive, and not being a creation of Congress, is relatively immune to Congressional review; it is the most secret of all U.S. intelligence agencies..... the NSA maintains no contact with the public or the press.*"[10] [Emphasis added]

These same illegal operations—not be found in the Constitution and never authorized by *We the People* or our duly-elected representatives to exist—are trying to overthrow our own government today. Maybe, just maybe, it's time to wake up and smell the coffee. There is a reason such

---

[9] *Walker, Samuel. Popular Justice: A History of American Criminal Justice,*
[10] *National Security Agency, Encyclopaedia Brittanica, Vol. 8, Micropaedia, p. 550*

rogue agencies were precluded from existence by our Founders, and any possible good they might have ever done is far outweighed by the evil now known to have been perpetrated by them.

No one is safe—even the President of the United States—as long as such rogue, unaccountable people can roam the globe murdering foreign leaders, starting wars and trafficking in drugs to support themselves.

Wanted: One Set of Large 'Cohones'—Preferably Used

There is no place in a free nation for such unconstitutional organizations with or without reasonable congressional oversight and review. They are illegal and have now proven beyond any doubt that they are far more dangerous to the nation than any protection they purport to offer it.

Taking out a sitting president? What on earth were the Progs thinking? Did they really think they could get away with it—or worse—will they yet get away with it by taking out the President and putting in their girl? We know law does not matter to them, so don't count on Vice-President Pence to be the next in line, just because the Constitution says so.

We need, and I believe finally have, a man with—I'll use the word 'courage'—to do something about this problem, but only if we give him some help.

Aside from proving themselves lethal to leaders at home and abroad, these unconstitutional groups are also unnecessary. Provision for appropriate, *constitutional* intelligence gathering, under the proper oversight of Congress, has always been available through the legal department of naval intelligence—and under that branch of government. Congress was intended to oversee this part of government, not the president.

Starting offensive wars, murdering foreign leaders, and training terrorists are not appropriate functions of a constitutional United States government. Such crimes have put the nation at risk by having been sanctioned and carried out by our Presidents over the past 70 years and it *must* stop.

The true purpose of these sixteen secretive spy agencies, and the military, according to author, John Perkins (who once served them) is to act on behalf of what he dubbed America's "*Corporatocracy*". He wrote, "*Our military is not a defender of democracy, but rather an armed guard for exploitive corporations.*"[11] The NSA, on the other hand, is here at home to spy on us. There is no excuse or constitutional authority for any of them.

Every president who has started a unilateral war or violated a treaty, to which the United States is a party, should have been impeached and removed from office. That would sadly include every president back to and including, Harry S. Truman. Until Congress or a president finds the courage to challenge these infringements on and violations of our Constitution, which have so endangered the nation, the United States will remain on a self-destructive course toward tyranny—the stated goal of the Progressives over a century ago.

It is the fabricated, often wholly-created conflicts started by these illegal agencies abroad, that have given government cause—and often, support from the public—to take our liberties in the name of 'safety.' Government purports that this is being done to protect the nation's citizens. Aside from being illegal, that is also distasteful, dangerous, and a very poor bargain.

Twentieth century writer and journalist, H.L. Mencken, wrote of this farce, "*The whole aim of practical politics is to keep the populace alarmed (and hence clamorous to be led to safety) by menacing it with an endless series of hobgoblins, all of them imaginary.*"

---

[11] Perkins, John. *The Secret History of the American Empire*, p. 291

Seventy years of immoral and flagitious skullduggery by the CIA and its 15 bastard sister agencies have created some real hobgoblins and bogeymen since Mencken's day, but stopping the overt acts which have caused this hatred of our nation is the surest way to end it, rather than piling on more of what caused it.

Cessante causa, cessat effectus. When the cause ceases, the effect ceases.

And while ending the bloody hell of *spy v. spy* and world wars may sound utopic, only the nation's so-called leaders have dragged us into them as revealed by recently discovered history. The nation was duped, tricked or spurred into the last century of wars by leaders doing so to serve the corporate interests and bankers who benefit from and rule the Progressive movement.

World War I? Cargo was intentionally exploded in the hull of the Lusitania rather than by a German torpedo (as was told to the public) sinking it and killing 195 Americans as a pretext to drag America into war. Why? Because the man who put Woodrow Wilson in the White House, Progressive millionaire, J.P. Morgan, was about to go under from funding England's war effort against the Germans.[12] All those young men died to save (and enrich) J.P., not the the English.

Pearl Harbor was used to drag us into WWII. President Roosevelt was warned 17 days in advance of the raid, but chose not to even give his officers or his own fellow-citizen soldiers and seamen warning, so he would have an excuse to declare war. *"The total number of military personnel killed was 2,335, including 2,008 navy personnel, 109 marines, and 218 army. Added to this were 68 civilians, making the total 2403 people dead. 1,177 were from the USS Arizona. The number of wounded came to 1,143 with 710 navy, 69 marines, and 364 army, as well as 103 civilians."*[13] Twenty-three sets of

---

[12] The Creature from Jekyll Island, by G. Edward Griffin. American Media. First published in 1994. 40th edition, 2010, p. 247

[13] https://visitpearlharbor.org/faqs/how-many-people-died-at-pearl-harbor-during-the-attack/

brothers died aboard the USS Arizona on December 7, 1941, as 37 confirmed pairs or trios of brothers were on that ship.[14] Why Roosevelt did it, I don't know. Perhaps to reward his backers with contracts or to follow the Progressive plan for world control and be its dominate leader, but I'm sure the parents of all those young men would have never forgiven him, had they known what he did. At least there were real threats to our part of the world in Europe, but Japan? No.

The "communist threat" in Vietnam? According to Professor Alfred W. McCoy in *"The Politics of Heroin in Southeast Asia"*—and later confirmed in Congressional testimony by General Richard Secord as well as Lt. Col. Oliver North—funding for the CIA comes largely from illegal trafficking in drugs. First it was only heroin, then more recently cocaine. The CIA was attempting to take over the Golden Triangle heroin trade from the French to fund their illegal operations, which McCoy states was the sole reason for our going in to Vietnam. More recently, the CIA used the War in Afghanistan for this purpose.[15]

"Weapons of mass destruction" in Iraq? Nonsense. They never found a one, but Halliburton and other Bush-Cheney allies found fortunes and are still there 17 years later making money.

"Terrorists"—Afghanistan, Pakistan, Ethiopia, and Somalia, to name just a few—well, you get the picture. Create a bogeyman, instill fear in the populace, and take their rights in the name of protection. A game as old as our nation, and as Benjamin Franklin once wrote of this practice, *"He who is willing to give up his freedoms for temporary safety, is deserving of neither."*

Change can come, with a return to constitutional government, and as Victor Hugo once wrote, *"Greater than the tread of mighty armies is an*

---

[14] https://www.history.com/news/5-facts-about-pearl-harbor-and-the-uss-arizona

[15] I have interviewed soldiers who were in charge of transporting raw opium to CIA labs in Lahore, Pakistan for heroin production to fund the CIA. Under Osama bin Laden, Afghan opium production was down to less that 2,200 hectares in 2002. After a decade of U.S. control, Afghan production was 1.25 times the world's average yearly usage—and it is now one of the cheapest drugs on the streets of America as a result, causing the greatest opioid addiction crisis in history.

idea whose time has come." The fruits of an Executive Branch exercising unconstitutionally granted powers are too bitter to bear much longer. It is time for a president with the courage to put the presidency back in its place—and force his co-equal branches of government to do the same. The time for this idea *has come.*

The majority of executive departments and agencies now under Executive control are either constitutional functions of Congress, the Judicial Branch, or are altogether unauthorized as duties of federal government. This can no longer be overlooked if we are to return to legitimate federal authority and a separation of powers.

Perhaps We Should Have Listened to Wise Old Ben Franklin

Of the 15 Executive departments, only the Department of the Treasury, Department of State, Department of Commerce (for international trade) and Department of Defense—and then only in time of declared war— are legitimate areas of executive power. The rest are without constitutional basis and/or have been self-granted by Executives acting outside their lawful authority.

Possibly the biggest mistake our Founders made was not listening to their oldest and possibly wisest member, Benjamin Franklin, when he proposed that the Executive Branch be run by a three-man committee. The difference such a small change could have made in our nation is unimaginable—the wars avoided, the temperance of ego-driven and politically-motivated decisions which have taken us from the path of liberty. The steadying hand of other opinions and a modicum of restraint would have changed history.

Perhaps one day *We the People* will have to have another Convention of States and implement this plan of Benjamin Franklin to save ourselves from the political collection of executive power which has done so much harm to our country. Take any election of the past century and imagine how much better off we would be by having the top three contenders as a committee, rather than just one person running the nation whose first loyalties were to his political party and staying in power rather than to *We the People*.

It would truly be a different, and in my opinion, a far better, kinder, and safer world.

Action Plan

By force of congressional action, confirm the invalidity of the Executive Order as a means of making law, and make such Executive legislation an impeachable offense. That should be added to the Convention of States agenda to get the attention of Congress as well.

Any agency of government, independent or quasi-independent department, commission or body with any authority, which was created outside of constitutional authority and the legislative process, must be assumed by Congress for liquidation, or conformation to a constitutionally authorized function of federal government found in Article I, Section 8. That would get rid of most of them.

Presidential authority over the military is clearly defined as only existing during time of declared war. Congress must reassert its constitutional authority over the military, and remove any Executive Branch control, except when the President assumes the title of Commander in Chief, during an officially and constitutionally declared war.

And finally, Congress must move to create Offices of Ombudsmen in every federal district as Article III courts—but have each Ombudsman elected by those within that district with no limitations or requirements other than that he or she reside within that district. This will not only benefit *We the People* when we're getting run over by rogues of government courts and agencies, but those in government itself who see criminal wrong-doing within the agencies that typically hold themselves above the law.

Rogues of government, for example, Deputy Attorney General, Rod Rosenstein, who has refused for almost a year to give over documents to Congress regarding his department's own illegal activities? One visit by Congressmen Trey Gowdy or Devin Nunes to their local DC District Office of Ombudsman could have taken care of that problem. Congress has constitutional oversight, which means that the Ombudsman could bring Rod Rosenstein before a grand jury and charge him criminally for violation of his constitutional duties—something the FBI and DOJ would never do to themselves.

This is an idea whose time has definitely come.

Chapter 9

WHAT DO WE DO ABOUT ANDY?

SUPPOSE you had a guy that put so many people in prison and out of work by lying, breaking the law, cheating, hiding the truth (and lying about that too) that they would completely fill a city the size of Danbury, Connecticut; or Lakewood, California; or Longview, Texas; or Cranston, Rhode Island?

The guy I'm talking about is so corrupt and despicable that the Supreme Court said so 9:0, which is almost unprecedented for them all to agree on anything. What do you do with such a guy who makes up laws that do not even exist, charges innocent people for violating them, sends them to prison, destroys companies with as many as 80,000 employees—for absolutely zero criminal conduct—and won't even say he's sorry?

Well, if you are part of the Soros-backed Progressive movement or one of their people in government, you promote him to Chief of The Criminal Fraud Division of the Department of Justice. Then, when an election does not go your way, you make him Chief Counsel of your attempt to frame and take down a duly elected President, using those same skills—lying, breaking the law, cheating, hiding the truth (and lying about that too).

Who is This Guy?

I'm speaking in particular about Andrew Weissman, but you could just as easily have picked more-or-less anyone in management of the FBI or the DOJ today and find a similar background of lawlessness. They do not work for us, they work for the so-called "Progressive" Movement and have no other loyalties.

Take Robert Mueller as another example—the man who after running the FBI, made a second career out of leading the witch-hunt against duly-elected President Donald Trump in an unprecedented and lawless set-up. Study the man Robert Mueller and you will learn that it is simply a continuation of his service to the Soros-backed Progressives and the evil they propose to do our country and Constitution.

This is the same Robert Mueller, who along with his co-conspirators, James Comey, Lois Lerner, and Rod Rosenstein, protected the Clinton machine bosses from being indicted under President George Bush, and later served the Clintons and Obamas, by allowing themselves and their agencies to be used in complete service to keeping power in the hands of the self-appointed elites rather than elected officials. [See pages 10-11]

But how long has Robert Mueller been so crooked and corrupt in their service? I was at the University of Virginia when Bob was there in law school, and he was reputed to be a stand-up guy. What happened to him?

The Progressives' ideology of Elitism and god-like powers promised its members is a siren-song for sure, especially to those like Soros (and Mueller) who are already convinced of it.

Mueller's history is very instructive also because it shows the seductive power of their indoctrination to turn any advantage—lawful or unlawful —to their own use and advancement. *"In Boston, Mueller was an Assistant*

U.S. Attorney in the U.S. Attorney's Office and then became the Acting U.S. Attorney from 1986 through 1987.

It was Mueller's actions during that time that raised questions about his role in one of the FBI's most controversial cases involving the FBI's use of a confidential informant that led to the convictions of four innocent men, who were sentenced to death for murders they did not commit."[1] Mueller's office, it was proven at the trial of this 'confidential informant' (Whitey Bulger), *"would inform Bulger of wiretaps and surveillance being conducted by law enforcement."*[2]

While Whitey Bulger worked for Mueller's team and under their protection, he is alleged to have murdered 16 people—and was warned by them when other law enforcement agencies were closing in to arrest him so he could escape justice. That ended in 2013 when he was caught in California by U.S. Marshals, but not with any assistance from Robert Mueller or his FBI, as Whitey was an embarrassment and evidence of what Mueller had done to advance himself and his own agenda. But it worked. Mueller became head of the FBI even though, *"On August 12, [2013]the jury convicted Bulger of 31 out of 32 counts in the indictment. As part of the racketeering charges, the jury convicted Bulger of the murders of 11 victims."*[3]

The lesson—under Progressivism at any rate is—the lower you are willing to go for them, the higher you can go in their government.

"Local law enforcement officials, the media, and some colleagues criticized Mueller and the FBI for what they believed was the bureau's role in covering up for the FBI's longtime dealings with mobster and informant James 'Whitey' Bulger,"[4] but his behavior since, including his attempts to set up

---

[1] https://saraacarter.com/questions-still-surround-robert-muellers-boston-past/ Three of those innocent men were sentenced to death in the electric chair.

[2] Ibid.

[3] https://en.wikipedia.org/wiki/Whitey_Bulger

[4] Ibid 34.

and take down a sitting president indicate there has been no improvement in either Bob's ethics or character since his days in Boston.

So what do we do about Andy, Bob, Rod, Lois, and the thousands of corrupt people now trying to depose a duly-elected president and obliterate our Constitution? How did these breeding grounds of criminal behavior come to be in the first place? More importantly, why has the Supreme Court suborned it in silence?

How Did We Get Here?

Let's start by looking at how the only Constitutional body mentioned in that question—the Supreme Court—allowed its own role to be changed.

For most of the first century of the nation's history as the United States, the Supreme Court was situated in the basement of the Capitol Building in an unused sub-committee room. That is how unimportant it was considered in a constitutional federal government.

They handled all federal appeals and cases but now, in their black robes, with enormous staffs for each of the nine judges, in their huge marble mansion, they handle an average of only 70 cases per year—far less than even a single public defender does in a small town. Maybe it's time to take their robes and put them back in the basement.

In fact, even the need for a federal judiciary in a government of such constitutionally limited powers was questionable to the Founders. The original plan had been to make the High Court a sub-department of Congress to roll out only in the rare instances where issues fell under its purview, such as boundary disputes between the States or to punish a counterfeiter. External affairs, such as piracy, or an American violator of the laws of other nations, were also its purview, but little more could be considered a federal issue.

The Judicial Branch was ultimately set apart by the Constitutional Convention under Article III, to act as a part of the checks and balances of government. It was initially a monitor of adherence to the Constitution by the Executive and Legislative branches. The Supreme Court did not hear or review a single case its first year to give some idea of how busy it was when the Constitution was in effect. The Court mainly monitored congressional legislation from the basement in the same building.

And that system worked well. Legislation was vetted for its compliance with the Constitution as it was being written, which had the effect of limiting mission creep by federal government up until the 1860s when the Court left its sub-committee room in the basement of Congress and moved into its own lavish quarters less than two blocks east of the Capitol.

Things have gone considerably downhill since then.

While the famous case of *Marbury v. Madison* in 1803 is credited with establishing the principle of judicial review, it was a *de facto* and intended result of working with Congress in close quarters under the same roof in the early days. The justices *prevented* unconstitutional legislation from becoming law in the first place. That simple system worked then, and could again.

Marbury v. Madison confirmed the principle, which already existed that, *"All laws which are repugnant to the Constitution are null and void,"* but now we have 314,000 laws that are repugnant to the Constitution, and all nine justices are clearly asleep on the job in the marble mansion.

What If?

Had the Supreme Court continued this practice of reviewing legislation prior to its passage, either informally or formally, the explosion of illegal government incursion into areas of the citizens' lives where it has no legitimate authority, could have been largely avoided. But it wasn't, and it wasn't because the court was stacked with Progressives from both parties, intent on destroying the constitution rather than upholding it.

We now have an illegal Federal Bureau of Investigation created as an executive tool for investigating political enemies and a Department of 'Justice' incapable of anything of the sort, a Congress that makes almost exclusively unconstitutional laws, and as long as the Tiger Shrimp are tasty at lunch, not a single Supreme Court justice seems to give a damn.

The Supreme Court's practice since its physical separation from the lawmakers in the 1860s has been one of review long after the passage of unconstitutional law, and only then after significant harm has been done by the offending statute. The odds of review by the High Court are a long shot at best today. In fact, it is 100:1

Of approximately 7,000 applications for *certiorari*, the Supreme Court hears roughly 70. With such miserable odds of illegal legislation or bad lower court decisions ever being challenged in the High Court, the Legislative Branch (and lower courts) have known little restraint.

The result of this wilful neglect and dereliction of duty by the Supreme Court has been the proliferation of 314,000 laws, almost all of which are *repugnant to the Constitution* as *Marbury* so eloquently put it, and the advent of a police state run by unelected "Progressives," complete with kangaroo courts and 'professional' prosecutors to enforce them. These courts are staffed almost exclusively by former prosecutors as their judges, which has been a recipe for disaster and made the United States the largest penal colony in world history as a result.

The 18,000+ police agencies that have mushroomed across post-constitutional America, employ hundreds of thousands of agents looking for (or creating) infractions of these 314,000+ mostly illegitimate federal laws, on a daily basis. The unconstitutional and seriously misnomered Department of Justice now has 94 offices scattered around the United States, staffed to the gills with largely-unsupervised young lawyers seeking convictions, by using constitutionally repugnant statutes and methods just like the leaders of their organization have now been revealed to do—even trying to takedown a duly elected president who is not to their liking—and all of which would make a third-world despot blush.

77.1% of the DOJ's victims are never allowed a moment of freedom to prepare their defense, as the Eighth Amendment in the Bill of Rights requires. The courts have re-interpreted this inalienable right to be an elective one, rendering it no longer a right at all.

Since the ridiculously named Bail Reform Act of 1984, whose "reform" was to eliminate the right to bail in most federal cases, all these Executive Branch U.S. Attorneys have to do to have their targets trapped and illegally detained is to claim to the court that the citizen is a "flight risk" or "a danger to the community." Taking no chances on fairness, they claim both in almost every case I have reviewed.

The victim is then held interminably, outside of statutory law (The Speedy Trial Act of 1974) as well as the Sixth Amendment (the right to a Public and Speedy Trial) until there is no alternative other than to negotiate a plea of guilt to often unconstitutional or uncommitted *crime* to end being illegally held in a dangerous and overcrowded county jail, where one often has to sleep on the floor, because all of the beds are taken.[5]

---

[5] The Wake County Jail of Senior District Court Judge W. Earl Britt in Raleigh, NC has 23 cells to each small cell block, but I have recorded as many as 63 extra men being forced to sleep on the floor in the pod's common space—because this judge and others in the Eastern District of North Carolina so rarely grant constitutionally required bail or realease. The equally dangerous Mecklenburg County Jail in Charlotte, NC has a similar problem because of Chief Western District Judge Francis D. Whitney's refusal to grant bail and often has more prisoners on the floors than in cells as well. In 2010, the jail was raided by federal authorities over its illegal activities, but those practices (and Judge Whitney's defiance of law) continue to this day.

It works—which is why 'Andy' and the gang do it—just like King George the tyrant did with his Tower of London. But in America, it is illegal under our Constitution, and we don't (yet) have a king.

By using the brutal methods of tyrants and thugs, the federal government has achieved a 98.6% conviction rate and filled every jail bed and most of their floor space across the nation with American citizens who have not been convicted by any court of law.

How Often Do They Get It Wrong?

Good question, and the courts themselves have answered it in a review of 5,760 capital cases—cases where they were going to kill the person— over a 23 year period between 1973 and 1996.[6]

The courts' findings of their own errors sounds so preposterous, I'll just quote from an article about it from, *The New Yorker*:

> '*A landmark Columbia Law School study of virtually every state and federal death-penalty appeal from 1973 to 1995 reported that "courts found serious, reversible error in nearly 7 of every 10 of the thousands of capital sentences that were fully reviewed during the period." There were so many mistakes, the study found, that after "state courts threw out 47% of death sentences due to serious flaws, a later federal review found 'serious error'—error undermining the reliability of the outcome—in 40% of the remaining sentences." Without federal habeas corpus, those serious errors would have gone unchecked. Instead of later being found not to deserve the death penalty, as happened in seventy-three per cent of the cases, or instead of being found innocent, as happened in nine per cent of the cases, these defendants likely would have been put to death.*'[7]

[Emphasis added]

---

[6] https://deathpenaltyinfo.org/summary-columbia-university-study-prof-james-s-liebman
[7] https://www.newyorker.com/news/news-desk/the-destruction-of-defendants-rights?intcid=mod-latest

The Progressive Answer

So what did they do, after learning that 'Andy' fucked up more than 7 out of every 10 times—even when he was going to kill the guy? The Department of 'Justice' proposed A.E.D.P.A.—the Anti-Effective Death Penalty Act—to Congress, which acted to suspend our Constitutional right of *habeas corpus* so no one would know about how horribly they did their jobs. Attorney and Progressive President Bill Clinton signed it into law—in 1996—the last year of the study. Things have gone considerably downhill since then I suspect, as the error rate certainly did not improve when our right to challenge court error was unlawfully taken from us.

Article 1, Section 9 is crystal clear—well, to anyone except lawyers and Congressmen apparently—as it states, "*The Privilege of the Writ of habeas corpus shall not be suspended, unless when in Cases of Rebellion or invasion the public Safety may require it.*," yet A.E.D.P.A. did just that.[Emphasis added]

Under A.E.D.P.A., the prisoner has only one year to file such a motion after a false or illegal conviction, which is usually before he or she even gets from detention in county jails to a prison to begin their sentence, and the strict limitations put on these generally poor, untrained people to figure out how to file a case in a federal district court is beyond all but the fewest.

About the only thing left that can be appealed is a court's complete lack of jurisdiction, but then—as I found out working on just such a case in North Carolina where a judge from another district two jurisdictions away poached it to get even with a prominent political enemy—10 appeals later, every court in the chain all the way to The U.S. Supreme Court simply refused to address the court's absence of jurisdiction to protect the reputation of their colleague.[8]

---

[8]Western District NC case 3:06-cr-74, was poached by Eastern District Senior Judge W. Earl Britt who

From working on over 400 criminal cases where 'Andy' was putting them away for years or decades instead of murdering the poor bastards, the rate of error actually exceeds '7 out of 10.' Law is violently broken in almost every case I've worked on, starting with the illegal detention mentioned earlier—which is how 'Andy' has set the world record for both highest rate of conviction—and the world's worst record of *getting it wrong*.

The Speedy Trial Act (18 U.S.C. §3161, et seq), is broken into sections. §3164(c), for example, demands the release of prisoners designated as "*high risk*" by the prosecutors if they are not tried within 90 days of arrest or arraignment, but I never once saw or heard of 'Andy' following that law and worked on cases where defendants had been held for five years and more, because they refused to take his 'plea' deal.

The definition of a "speedy trial" in §3161(c)(l) of the Act is 70 days between arrest and the beginning of the trial. Federal law and the Constitution are violated if the prisoner is not tried within that time, plus any excludable delays, yet this has not happened in even one of the hundreds of cases I've been involved with or reviewed.

Further, §3162(a)(2) requires the indictment to be dismissed "*upon motion of the defendant*" if the 70-day clock is violated, but defendants are not only never advised of this right, attorneys are now sanctioned in many U.S. District Courts for filing such a motion.[9]

---

illegally adjudicated it in violation of federal law and Constitution. After 10 appeals, no court has ever addressed the Eastern District court and judge's lack of personal or subject matter jurisdiction. The defendant unlawfully spent 7 years in prison as a result, though never convicted in or by any court of jurisdiction. The offending Judge, W. Earl Britt is still on the federal bench—at age 86—and has been found to have committed these same unconstitutional acts in several other cases, but has never been rebuked or suspended.

[9]In 2010, Western District NC Judge and former U.S. Attorney, Francis D. Whitney, called a conference of all attorneys registered in his district court and warned them that if they filed a motion under §3162 or were found to have advised their clients of this law, they would be sanctioned. Whitney was elevated to Chief Judge of the Western District of North Carolina, replacing his fellow prosecutor, Judge Joseph Conrad, who had been forced out of the Western District previously as U.S. Attorney for forcing and coercing defendants into illegal plea bargains. As seems to be the case with Progressives, the worst become the highest. Conrad became Chief Judge in the same court which refused his illegal plea bargains as prosecutor, only to be followed by Judge Whitney as Chief Judge, who threatened attorneys who followed the law and vigorously defended their clients with sanctions. And there is no meaningful oversight of these rogue judges except 'peer review.' Of 1,000 complaints filed by attorneys against lawless federal judges that were reviewed by Congress, not a single judge was found guilty, suspended, or punished by his or her 'peers.' *Justice Restored: 10 steps to end mass incarceration in America*, by Howell W. Woltz, (2017), p. 69, 105.

The National Association of Criminal Defense Lawyers estimated in 2009 that 75% of the prison population in America was wrongfully convicted, largely due to the failure of federal government to follow its own laws—though the criminal defense lawyers have been complicit in allowing this to happen. If they were doing their jobs, such a number would be impossible—though I understand, as there is no Ombudsman to hear them.

If that number (75%) is right—or the courts' own admission of error and actual innocence rate is close—that means that 75% of the 71 million Americans ruined since 1973 by 'Andy'— 53,250,000 American citizens— have been wrongfully disenfranchised by the Progs since I was in college. Such numbers are holocaustic.

It is truly heartbreaking. When one considers that many of the laws under which these convicted citizens were charged and imprisoned (or executed) were in areas over which government had no authority to begin with, it goes from heartbreaking to disgusting.

Well, One Night We Were Getting Drunk With the President....

So where did we get this poorly named Department of Justice that is run by actual criminals operating under color of law? A descendant of President Ulysses S. Grant once told me (over drinks in the Union League Club sitting under his ancestor's portrait) the family lore of how Grant and some members of the Republican post-Civil War government came up with the idea over a late night drinking game in the White House before the defeated southern States were allowed to re-enter the Union. The intention (and result) of founding this unconstitutional department was to usurp as much of the power of the federal Judiciary before the

Southern States returned, greatly increase it, and put it under the control of the Executive Branch, where it remains to this day.[10]

The Department of Justice was officially created in March of 1870, but never voted on by the full Congress. While the Civil War was fought over a claim that States had no right to secede, their votes were not allowed when it counted most—a serious, if not unlawful, hypocrisy. This agency, though prohibited as a duty or power of federal government, was placed under the portfolio of then-Attorney General, Amos T. Akerman, who reported directly to President Grant.

This was nothing short of a power play intended to disrupt the balance and separation of powers in favor of the Executive. It has enabled political donors and corporations who give large amounts of money, to direct the changes they wanted in government by force of law and influence, through politically motivated attacks on others—just as is still being done by unelected deep state Progs and operatives against the president today, even though he is technically their boss.

There is no authorization in Article II of the U.S. Constitution empowering the Executive Branch to control such a department, and the statistics readily confirm its true purpose. Nationally famous attorney, Harvey A. Silverglate, revealed the endemic corruption and abuse of power within the Bush and Obama Executive Department in 2009, in his landmark book, *Three Felonies a Day: How the Feds Target the Innocent*." (Encounter Books, NY). He cited a study which can only lead to one conclusion about the true purpose for this department, and its unauthorized inclusion as an Executive power:

"Study by Professors Donald C. Shields and John F. Cragan found that between 2001 and 2007 the D.O.J. [Department of Justice]

---

[10] *While it is widely believed that the Department of Justice is under the purview of the Judicial branch of government, it is not. 28 U.S.C. §501 Executive department, states: "The department of Justice is an executive department of the United States at the seat of Government." (Added Pub. L.89-554, §4(c), Sept. 6, 1966, 80 Stat.611.)*

*opened investigations into seven times more Democratic public of-
ficials than Republican. The professors concluded that the odds of
this discrepancy being a random occurrence were one in ten thousand."*

When the Obama Administration came to power, the numbers of Republicans being attacked over Democrats, simply reversed. Revelations
of the deep-state operatives targeting non-progressive fund-raising organizations while protecting the Clinton Foundation and Soros-backed
entities should prove that this Executive department is nothing more
than a blunt political tool, abused by both parties. It is not one of justice, nor was it intended to be.

Has It Ever Worked Right?

Yes. Not the unconstitutional 'Department of Justice', but our system
of justice once worked well and was the most respected on earth, as no
prosecution could be brought against a citizen by any branch of federal
government until it was reviewed by the Attorney General's office and
confirmed to be under the purview of federal power and authority. Then,
the party wishing to bring the charge was required to *prove* that sufficient
evidence existed for a conviction, prior to a prosecution ever being initi-
ated.

The system of today, as confirmed by former Eastern District NC U.S.
Attorney Samuel T. Currin (in an interview after leaving office) is now
the reverse. The target—usually a political opponent or a poor black or
brown person—is chosen. His or her life is put under the investigators'
microscope using any means necessary including wiretaps, collection of
e-mails and data, solicitations of informants to lie—anything, legal or
illegal, as no one is watching them—until a potential violation of one of

the 314,000 laws is found. If none is found, they are charged with the 'intent' of committing a crime (conspiracy).

A grand jury is convened—in secret, of course, to prevent truth from being told or challenged—and the prosecutor lies, cajoles, or barks at the grand jury chosen by their own operatives until a True Bill of Indictment is issued, which borders on 100% of all cases presented. The target is then arrested, held without bail in the most horrible circumstances imaginable, until he or she 'confesses' and another notch is carved into the prosecutor's belt. Of 1,000 who are collected by the system, only the 14 richest or most prominent go free.

The purpose of the onerous historical procedure that existed before the advent of the Department of 'Justice' was designed to prevent false, malicious or politically-motivated attacks on citizens. It also acted as a component of the overall checks and balances of constitutional government. The citizens were the beneficiaries of those protections and they are the losers as a result of their disappearance under the Department of Justice's reign.

Prior to this unconstitutional tinkering by President Grant and his Reconstruction Republican Congress, the Attorney General did not even head up an executive department. He was an advisor to—and drinking buddy— with the President, as well as representing the government as plaintiff or defendant in cases before the Supreme Court.

Now, the Attorney General today has 94 offices (including his headquarters) stocked to the gills with mostly young, over-empowered, under-supervised U.S. government Attorneys capable of targeting any person, political organization, corporation or institution in America, and destroying them at will. If that sounds too harsh, it was the "Andy" named above who personally did this to corporations such as Enron, Arthur Anderson, and Merrill-Lynch—all convictions from which were overturned as being illegal, but only after costing tens of thousands of people their jobs, reputations, and in many cases, their freedom.

And what happened to 'Andy' for committing all of these crimes just so he could win convictions and get notches in his belt? Well, instead of being prosecuted, he was made boss. They put him in charge of all the other young Turks to teach them his very effective but completely illegal methods. Lie, cheat, do anything you have to to win (and then lie about that).

The results of creating this massive department with the power to prosecute and destroy have been disastrous for the nation and the disruption of the balance and separation of powers may yet prove fatal. The Department of Justice was the genesis of the police state that exists today and its arrogance and power are so great that it is trying to take out the Presidency they once served, in nothing short of a *coup d'etat*—though not a one of them was ever elected.

So How Far Back Does This Go?

The Supreme Court seems to have been oblivious to all of this— if not complicit in it—ever since President Lincoln let them out of the broom closet in the basement of the Capitol and gave them their own digs. They certainly did not challenge President Lincoln after he ignored their ruling in *Ex parte Merryman*, where it was decided that only Congress had the power to suspend the privilege of *habeas corpus* (Lincoln did so unilaterally in 1861 by Executive Order One, as previously mentioned) and it did not challenge President Grant when he illegally formed an Executive Department of "Justice" that was wholly unconstitutional, or President Teddy Roosevelt when he illegally created his FBI, or for that matter, President Truman over his CIA and NSA or the others on their 15 other illegal spy outfits.

Perhaps the justices feared being put back in the broom closet in the basement of Congress and chose handsome surroundings to doing their job. We'll never know their reasoning, but the results are clear—they're too comfortable to cause waves, so it's time we woke them up with term limits too.

Regardless, their timid tone was set. The Supreme Court has continued its timorous ways since Lincoln's days with one notable exception known as the "Switch in time that saved nine" scandal in 1937. That event could be said to have ended the Court's independence as a branch of government for all intents and purposes.

Bolder Than Fiction

The Hughes Court was set to reject President Franklin Roosevelt's New Deal legislation as unconstitutional, which according to Article I, Section 8, it was and still is—all of it. When Roosevelt threatened to liquidate the justices' voting power by increasing their number (and packing it with six Progressives), Justice Hughes folded opposition and capitulated.

Article III does not specifically state that there must be nine judges on the Supreme Court, so Roosevelt's threat was very real (since limited by statute). His additional judges would undoubtedly have been confirmed by his party which controlled Congress.

But it is Time for The Court To Be Supreme

The Judicial Branch needs to step up and reestablish itself, starting at the head. Article III does not require or even contemplate Supreme Court Justices being attorneys. Many of our greatest justices and judges have not been formally trained in law, including the Supreme Court's Fourth Chief Justice, John Marshall, who is credited with establishing its purpose and course. More importantly, the principle author of the

Constitution, James Madison, whose document is all that is supposed to inform their judgments, was not an attorney either.[11] So why does the Bar only want lawyers? To keep their power. That's all.

The sole purpose of the Supreme Court is to keep the nation within the boundaries of Mr. Madison's Constitution (our contract), so this can hardly be a job which requires a law degree, obviously, as *its principle author, James Madison, was untrained in law.* That is why the Constitution is so easy to read and understand—as was the Founders' intent. Remember that they had to sell this idea to the people, which is why they chose the plain-speaking Virginian to write it instead of any of the attorneys in their midst.

Following rather than 'interpreting' the document is a job for sensible people who have studied our Founders' intent and care about their nation and its freedoms rather than attorneys. James Madison's words are extraordinarily simple and clear. As I've written in other books, '*it takes an attorney to misinterpret the Constitution, and nine of them in black robes to completely ignore it,*' so perhaps its time we tried putting some citizens with common sense on the High Court instead of legal hacks who can find words (like 'corporation' or 'democracy') in the document that are not there.

The system today has become so perverted under the custody and care of lawyers that it is unrecognizable as American justice. An excellent example of the most extraordinarily harmful (and unlawful) statutes are the outrageous Reagan-era conspiracy laws, ostensibly passed at the prompting of Department of Justice attorneys as a temporary measure to be used against Mafia bosses, but now used in 90% of all federal cases as suspenders. Why? Because there is no defense against a charge of conspiracy. That is why 'Andy' uses it in almost every case. Civilized nations

---

[11] *While Gouverneur Morris, John Blair, and Thomas Jefferson (via correspondence from his duties in France) did have legal training and great input into the content and wording of the U.S. Constitution, James Madison, a non-lawyer, is recognized as its principle author*

do not have such laws due to their potential for abuse, and in the wrong hands—like Andy's—this horrible crime of thought can be lethal.

Further, conspiracy is an inchoate (incomplete) crime of thought. It is not the commission of a crime, it is *thinking about committing one* that prosecutors had Congress outlaw. No overt act is required in order to be guilty and any two immunity hunters, known or unknown to government's target(s), can tell Andy that their fellow citizen *thought* about committing a crime and he or she will face more time in prison in many cases, than if they had committed the crime itself—while Andy's snitch gets an enormous break in his or her sentence for lying for him.

And while these real criminals—Comey, Brennan, Clapper, Sztrok, Page, Weissman, McCabe, and of course, the many other 'Andys' we don't yet know about, go uncharged, unconvicted and unpunished, sentences for murder, rape, robbery and aggravated assault—violent crimes—under their rule now average just 49 months in prison, while a conviction for this vague crime of thought—*conspiracy,* now used in almost every case, is often for decades.

Now add in the unlawful creation of a "Federal Bureau of Investigation" invented in 1907 to service Progressives by fabricating charges against their enemies[12] and support Andy in his false prosecutions, and you have the recipe for what we have today—lawlessness in government, under color of law—capable of taking down even a duly-elected president using wholly illegal means—and for nothing.

The Obama Administration and its Progressive puppets in the CIA, FBI, NSA, DOJ, and State Department are now known to have planted at least one spy in the Trump camp (University of Cambridge professor, Stefan Halper), set up banned Russian attorney Natalia Veselnitskaya—who denied any connection to the Russian government—to be issued

---

[12] https://www.washingtonpost.com/local/crime/fbi-overstated-forensic-hair-matches-in-nearly-all-criminal-trials-for-decades/2015/04/18/39c8d8c6-e515-11e4-b510-962fcfabc310_story.html?noredirect=on\&utm_term=.543312844485

an Obama Administration CIA and State Department-approved visa to enter the country to help with the Brennan, Comey, and Rosenstein set-up at Trump Towers—who later claimed she *did* represent Russian government interests; and finally putting 13 Trump-hating Progressives —all Democrats—in a campaign under Bob Mueller and Andy to destroy the president. Now that is a real conspiracy.

These same bad actors of government planted as the "investigators" of this alleged collusion between Trump and the Russians, are many of the same actors who illegally fabricated it—by actually colluding with Russians to do it.

It would be daunting trying to write fiction in America at a time such as this when the Progressive Movement is doing such outrageous things in reality. That same story as fiction would be deemed unbelievable and no publisher would touch it.

So what about DNI, FBI, CIA culprits James Clapper, James Comey and John Brennan's actual co-ordination with real Russian spies and the Obama State Department to create the fake dossier paid for by the Democratic National Committee and the Clinton campaign to then take to a FISA court along with multiple misstatements and outright lies to get permission to spy on then-citizen Trump and his campaign? We need to throw Rod Rosenstein in as well for signing the knowingly false FISA request, but do they and Hillary Clinton and John Podesta actually get off for doing what they falsely alleged against then-candidate Trump?

And even worse, who is then duped into delivering this *"salacious and unverified"* trash (as admitted and described by one of the people behind it, FBI leaker, James Comey) to give cover for the criminals in the deep state? Soros-backed progressive Republican Senator John McCain! Yes. This is stranger than fiction. It reminds me of an old poem I once read and committed to memory:

> *"In Libyan fable it is told, that once an eagle, stricken by a dart, upon examining the fashion of its shaft, exclaimed: 'Not by the hands of others, but by our own feathers are we now smitten.' "*

Sorry, Senator McCain. Trump was right again. You're only considered or known as a hero because you *surrendered* to the Communists in Vietnam. I wonder what the real heroes who refused surrender and fought them would think of that and your later surrender to the Progressive Soros camp to sell out the President of the United States and head of your own party?

Sounds like surrender is what you do, Senator McCain, and that does not make you a hero. The fact that the people you have sold out to all your life are the Communists, Socialists, and Progressives, who wanted to destroy your country, Sir, with any due respect, that makes you a traitor, not a hero.

It's Time to Take Them All Down, Andy First

What about a conspiracy to illegally depose a U.S. President? The only time a charge of conspiracy should be allowed in my opinion is when it involves government employees acting under color of law, such as in the Comey/McCabe/Mueller/Clapper/Brennan/Ohr/Page/Sztrok/Rosenstein/Weissman/Clinton/Podesta (and McCain) conspiracy to take down a sitting president.

Even the nation's closest neighbors, Canada and The Bahamas, refuse to extradite any citizen to the United States if the charge is for an alleged "conspiracy," as it is an immoral and indefensible law, which is also so unconstitutionally vague that no one can know it is being violated, nor can the defendant prove innocence. But conspiracy is a valid charge under 18 U.S.C. §§241 and 242 against these bandits, because these criminals are government employees knowingly and willingly violating the constitutional rights of a citizen as part of government, and doing so under color of its law.

Further, the non-government members of the conspiracy who aided and abetted in these crimes can also be charged and imprisoned for participating in the violation of rights under color of law, even if they are not actually in the government. This could include indicting, for example, Comey's friend, Columbia University professor, Daniel Richman, whom Comey asked to leak classified information to the press, and University of Cambridge professor, Stefan Halper, who acted as the FBI's spy in the Trump campaign, as co-conspirators.

And from listening to the news tonight....that list is growing. Chuck and Nancy better start pushing to build a new federal prison with golf courses and a Starbucks, cause it looks like its going to be full of their own—and maybe them too.

Start at the Beginning—Restore the Grand Jury System

This entire criminal process has deteriorated from beginning to end under the Department of Justice and the political hacks who run it. The constitutional grand jury process, which was created to protect the citizen from wrongful prosecutions from ever happening, has been transformed into a secretive affair which all but insures it. Sinister deeds and evil in every shape have full swing behind those closed doors today, to paraphrase Jeremy Bentham.

Targets of these inquisitions are no longer allowed to even have an attorney—which completely defies the Sixth Amendment guarantee of such a right in any criminal prosecution. False evidence and compensated witnesses scripted to lie by government prosecutors—such as was done by Andrew Weissman in most of his cases and more or less all of them today—are presented with impunity (and self-granted immunity). Transcripts are not allowed their victims where those misdeeds and misconduct might be exposed publicly.

The targets of these illegitimate courts are often not allowed to even be present themselves to raise a defense or contest government's fabrications, which also stands in clear opposition to what the Sixth Amendment was designed to prevent and in violation of its protections.

In today's Department of Justice system, this grand jury *show* is the closest 95% of government's victims will ever get to a trial though the Sixth Amendment still requires all criminal defendants *"the right to a speedy and public trial, by an impartial jury of the State and district where-in the crime shall have been committed."* Today's grand jury is a rubber stamp affair where it said that a prosecutor can *"indict a ham sandwich."* Andrew Weissman 'Andy' indicted and/or destroyed an entire city-size population without law, due process, and in violation of both. This same dirtbag is now part of the conspiracy to destroy the President of the United States, using the same unlawful means that cost him a 9:0 smackdown from the Supremes, if we don't do something to stop them first.

Next, End Plea Agreements

19 out of 20 of federal government's victims are forced to take a plea agreement via extortion, threats, intimidation and/or incarceration of their loved ones. Compare that 95% plea rate to the Sixth Amendment demand that *"In all* [100% of] *criminal prosecutions, the accused shall enjoy the right to a speedy and public trial, by an impartial jury of the State and district wherein the crime shall have been committed."* [comment added]

These coerced agreements 'Andy' forces on his victims are binding on the citizen but not on government, and in my years of writing about this constitutional anomaly, I have rarely seen the federal government keep any of the bargains it made to lure the citizen into signing away years of his or her life by ratting out their fellow citizens. I only hope the FBI/DOJ/CIA/NSA co-conspirators now trying to take down the president get to taste their own medicine before the system is repaired by their target, President Donald J. Trump (which a White House committee of 20 Democrats, Republicans, and Independents representing judicial reform interests from around the nation is presently doing).

No More 'Immunity' for Lawbreaking Judges and Prosecutors

Worse, and due to the protections given government criminals like Weissman, McCabe, Sztrok, et al, since 1967, prosecutors and judges who commit these crimes against *We the People*, are immune from prosecution for their own violations of law and Constitution. They are above the law, by self-granted judicial law, which is itself a violation of the Equal Treatment Clause (Amendment Fourteen). This anomaly came about due to a string of court decisions beginning with *Pierson v. Ray* in 1967, not by legislation. In other words, the courts granted themselves and their prosecutors immunity. Judges and prosecutors *suffer no penalty for violating the law and rights of We the People while performing their duties in our name.* Until this changes, 'Andy' will continue breaking the law with impunity. Thomas Jefferson once again warned of this happening:

> *"The Judiciary of the United States is the subtle corps of sappers and miners constantly working under ground to undermine the foundations of our confederated fabric."*
>
> *(1820)*
>
> *"...the Federal Judiciary; an irresponsible body (for impeachment is only a scarecrow), working like gravity by night and day, gaining*

> *a little to-day and a little tomorrow, and advancing its noiseless*
> *step like a thief, over the field of jurisdictions, until all shall be*
> *usurped from the States, and the government of all be consolidated*
> *into one....”*
>
> *(1821)*

Jefferson's admonitions were clear and this is why historians and constitutional scholars should be on the Supreme Court in balance with lawyers to prevent further lawlessness and *‘noiseless step[s] like a thief,’* by High Court members of the Bar, vested in this horrible *status quo*. Allowing judges and prosecutors to continue escaping punishment for the violation of constitutional rights, is a crime in itself. Non-lawyer jurists and justices would stop such constitutional anomalies, rather than ignoring and/or supporting them because they are "brother counsel" and members of the same illegally granted monopoly known as ‘the Bar.’

And I challenge anyone to tell me why an attorney needs to interpret a plain spoken document written in words that anyone living in the late 1780s in America could read and understand. Literacy rates went down after ‘mandatory public education’ laws were passed, beginning in 1851, so the citizens of pre-Constitution America could read it better than we can today after government schooling, but the point is this—don't let them prevent common sense on the bench, just because it might upset the legal class (and monopoly) that brought us to this horrific point.

The Blame For This Part is Clearly on the Monopoly

A Bar-licensed lawyer sat on the bench as judge in these 7+ out of 10 cases cited earlier, where tens of millions of defendants were illegally sentenced to death and prison between 1973 and 1996. Another "brother counsel" member of the Bar was the prosecutor who illegally charged that citizen and sent him or her to death, only to find in review that 9% of them were innocent and 70% of the trials were illegal—which was known to many of those prosecutors in the grand jury stage when the evidence was falsified or they had hidden exculpatory information from the grand jury. A licensed member of the Progressive-founded and run Bar was also sitting at the defense table and allowed these millions of their fellow citizens to be wrongfully imprisoned or murdered by the state, instead of doing their duty and vigorously defending them against the two government prosecutors (the one on the bench acting like an objective judge and the one at the bar violating them)—instead of sucking up to 'brother counsel'.

And it was these same lawyers and their Progressively-run monopoly who begged Congress to pass A.E.D.P.A. so they could no longer be found out as 'Andy' fuck-ups via constitutionally guaranteed *habeas corpus*. They chose to suspend it instead.

Suppose the duty of meat inspection was given over to a private guild by the State. No one else was allowed to inspect meat or they would go to jail for "practicing meat inspection without a license" from the guild, and the guild severely policed and enforced their monopoly over 'meat inspection'.

But it came to be known that the guild's inspectors were not only being wildly careless about their job—they were in fact, flouting the code of inspection so badly, that at all levels of the industry, 83% of the people who ate the meat they inspected—were either made sick for life or died —but this had been allowed to go on for decades.

Question. Would you let this private guild keep its monopoly over meat inspection in spite of its incredibly horrifying record? Would you further ignore the law and eliminate the public's right to have the meat checked by another inspector to see if it was bad, to prevent your incompetence from being publicly known, even if it continued to kill and sicken those you were granted the monopoly to protect?

If you answered yes, to either of these questions, you are most likely a lawyer, and if you answered yes to both, you are a Progressive one.

"So what if they die or spend a few decades in the hospital because of us," says one meat inspector guild member to the other. "We have our own inspectors and different rules, so we never get sick ourselves. That's all that matters. They're just 'deplorables' anyway, aren't they?"

And with this information now proven by the courts themselves on how horribly corrupt and incompetent their meat inspector lawyers of bench and bar in America actually are, how can we allow government to limit our courts to being run by the Progressive monopoly? It is clearly made up of such incredible incompetents, that we do ourselves a disservice by allowing them to have a monopoly on the practice of our laws—and certainly on having a death grip on our courts!

They will ruin our country if we continue letting them run our courts —especially the High one—which is not charged with making up laws or even 'interpreting' the Constitution—they are only required to follow the plain spoken words in it.

Jefferson's prophecies have come to pass. The oppression of the U.S. government and its federal judiciary is far worse than any ever beheld under King George III of England. America's prison population stands in evidence. With less than 5% of the world's population, we have roughly 25% of its prisoners, thanks to unethical prosecutors like Andrew Weissman ('Andy') who are above the law and as with him, corrupt prosecutors are promoted and often end up sitting as the judges who allow the overt corruption to continue (like Judges Britt, Conrad, and Whitney in my own home state—the most lawless have become the 'Chiefs' in their federal districts).

Jury Rights

The final insult and injury to *We the People* in the judicial arena has been the virtual elimination of jury powers under Prog rule. Under the Constitution, these powers are *unlimited and they still exist*, but Progressive Bar-ruled judges at all levels tell juries the opposite in their instructions. There is no other way to state what these courts are doing other than that they are lying to the jurors about their rights and powers, which should be the cause for overturn of every conviction in which this was done—and the immediate removal of that judge for bad behavior.

In my opinion, judges acting outside of lawful authority and function should not only be removed, but criminally prosecuted. The North Carolina Judges I investigated, such as EDNC Judge Britt (Democrat), WDNC Judge Whitney (Republican) and WDNC Judge Conrad (also Republican) have violated so many laws and constitutional provisions that they themselves should spend the rest of their lives in prison with their victims.

This has happened because American citizens are no longer taught their rights in government schools and few take the time to learn them. Government and courts clearly no longer enforce them, and the credit for the corrosive tactic of failing to inform jurors of their rights falls to the judges, but guilt must be shared by sycophantic lawyers and Congress—comprised of far too many attorneys and former prosecutors—who have allowed the foul practice to go unchallenged. As Jefferson also said of the Congressional power (and duty) to remove such judges, *"Impeachment is scarcely a Scarecrow."*

A decision made by a jury is unreviewable, for any reason. This ultimate power was retained by *We the People* as a safeguard against the tyranny we now face, but not knowing one's rights makes this power meaningless and of no value to anyone. A juror in a trial is more powerful than any judge, legislator, or even the President of the United States, but few know it. Putting monopoly members in black robes and on raised daises (for the short ones) is nonsense. Give me a non-monopoly sensible citizen as judge, with common sense in a plaid shirt and jeans, rather than dressing them up as something they are not.

I am required to respect and show obeisance to people so stupid that they get their job wrong "7 out of 10" times and 9% of the people they kill—almost one in ten— were provably innocent when they started the process? Not hardly. The system must change and the Progressive Bar Association that was illegally given a monopoly on who can discuss the People's law, needs to be disbanded. They have clearly not performed and they have the blood and lives of 52,000,000 of their fellow citizens on their hands.

When you get it wrong 7 out of 10 times and put 9% of your innocent victims to death—you deserve no pomp, circumstances, or respect. You deserve a penalty yourself, and the Clinton-era suspension of constitutional *habeas corpus* now protects these criminals in black robes and pinstripe suits from being outed—and results in more deaths and imprisonment of innocent people.

Further, jurors in constitutional courts are also the real judges. The citizen on the bench is just the referee. Jurors have the right, power, and duty to judge not only the facts in the case, *but whether the law itself is valid —or not.* The only power a judge has over a juror is that person's ignorance about his or her own unlimited authority. The judgment of a jury is above question or challenge by the court.

This is an important part of the foundation of the balance of powers as well as the legislators' best means of feedback from *We the People* when unacceptable laws are passed. If juries refuse to convict defendants under bad or unconstitutional law, which is called *jury nullification*, it sends a message to Congress or the legislature that it has erred by passing it.

Judges and government are powerless to do anything about such decisions, so the Progressive-controlled Bar Association has mandated to its members that they must lie to the jurors about their power over recent decades, to prevent lawful *nullification*. The mere mention of jury rights in a courtroom today will earn a lawyer a citation for contempt of court. Such courts are contemptible, as case law on this question was once clear:

> *"The jury has an unreviewable and unreversible power.... to acquit in disregard of the instructions on the law given by a trial judge."*
>
> *U.S. v. Dougherty, 473 F 2d 1113, 1139 (1972)*

Refusing to convict citizens under bad or unconstitutional law sends a clear message to the legislators that they have gone too far. This process of jury nullification caused the repeal of unconstitutional legislation such as The Alien and Sedition Acts (1798), The Fugitive Slave Act (1850), and other blights on the American conscience. It will hopefully save the nation from the *conspiracy* laws one day, once jurors again know of their powers to nullify 'repugnant' laws by refusing to convict their fellow citizens who are attacked under them.

Judicial instructions to the jury, as recently as my own teenage years accompanying my attorney grandfather, H. Osler Woltz, Sr., to court, still included the right to nullify, so these despicable changes are quite recent.

Judge's jury instructions in the Surry County courthouse of North Carolina in the 1960s were as follows:

> *"It is not only your power to decide the facts in this case, but to rule on the law itself. If the law itself is not in keeping with your own conscience, your values, or those of your community, it is within your power to set this man free."*

In Maryland, as recently as the 1980s, juries were advised by judges, they were not required to follow their instructions. In a 1967 jury instruction from a murder trial recently in the news due to being overturned, the judge stated, *"You, under our system, in criminal cases are at liberty to disagree with the court's interpretation of the law. You shall determine what the law is and then apply the law to the facts as you find them to be."*

Such honest instructions must return to the courtrooms of the United States. Jury nullification is the ultimate check and balance on government power. The Judicial Branch was to be controlled by *We the People* and our juries, not the government—or some unelected monopoly club of proven incompetents. That control must return to us.

The judicial powers of prosecution at the federal level must also be wrested from unelected U.S. Attorneys, and investigations should return to state and local agencies that are accountable. Open, fair, grand juries, under the control of *We the People,* prosecuted and investigated by *elected* authorities rather than political appointees is where that power constitutionally lies. The courts are the People's venue and their protection against government, not a tool for federal politicians and their political minions (or donors from their sanctioned monopolies) to use to oppress and imprison us.

Action Plan

We should start by re-establishing Supreme Court preview of all congressional legislation for compliance with the U.S. Constitution prior to its enactment as a safeguard against further trespass by Congress into areas outside of constitutionally listed federal powers.

Next, the Department of Justice should be removed from the Executive Branch immediately. No such power is granted under Article II of the Constitution and Congress had no power under Article I, Section 8 to create it as a department or added purview of the Executive Branch, especially without allowing all States to vote on it.

Next, we must put an end to federal prosecutions for violations of laws which are not specifically authorized by the United States Constitution as a function of federal government to enforce. The Kafkaesque 'conspiracy' statutes must be the first to go. Either a crime was committed or it was not. Putting people in prison for thinking about committing a crime is Sci-Fi nonsense, not valid law.

Close the 93 United States Attorney's Offices around the United States and return to the constitutional practice of justifying a federal prosecution prior to its initiation. The federal courts were never intended to be used for criminal prosecutions. Other than piracy on the high seas and against the laws of other nations; or counterfeiting federal securities and money, such criminal justice was to be the purview of the States.[13]

End the private monopoly of State and Federal Bar Associations, or give them public service as prosecutors—one case each—on a rotating basis. No more 'professional' prosecutors with no professional ethics and unaccountability. A private prosecutor has to return to private life amongst those he served and accused, which keeps the system fair.

Restore the sanctity of the venerable grand jury process where it is open, public, and no citizen can be indicted without having the opportunity to present his or her side, confront government's witnesses, and be represented by an attorney. There is no place for secrecy in the American judicial process and no (legal) excuse for it.

Require jury rights and the power of nullification to be part of every instruction given by the courts at both State and federal levels once again and encourage jurors to shut down bad laws by refusing to convict, as is their intended purview and power.

---

[13] Treason is also the province of the federal Courts, but it is listed under Article III as a power of the Judiciary to control. Congress's power to declare its punishment is granted as a federal power under Article III, Section 3 (Judicial Powers), but not the authority to implement laws regarding it.

Start a grassroots movement to pressure Presidential candidates to put constitutional scholars and historians on the Supreme Court, to balance the corrosive effect the legal profession has had on that institution. James Madison was not an attorney, and one is not required to interpret his words.

Chapter 10

BRING JOHNNY HOME

THE United States military is a difficult subject to address. For the most part, Americans are proud of their military and any question regarding the scope and size of our vast military presence around the globe is considered tantamount to treason.

But this book is about truth and what the United States was meant to be, not the propaganda we've been taught by those who have controlled it for the past century.

The author of the Constitution, James Madison, considered *a standing army* such as we now have, to be the most dangerous threat to liberty possible. The author of the Declaration of Independence, Thomas Jefferson, considered it second only to the dangers of a privately owned central bank issuing the public's currency.

We now have both—the largest standing army in the world and the biggest private central bank in human history

Madison wrote:

> *"Of all the enemies to public liberty war is, perhaps, the most to be dreaded because it comprises and develops the germ of every other.*

War is the parent of armies; from these proceed debt and taxes.... known instruments for bringing the many under the domination of the few.... No nation could preserve its freedom in the midst of continual warfare."

But The Progs Would Not Listen to Madison

Since the end of World War II, the United States has fought roughly 180 engagements. The nation has been in a state of continual warfare, some public, many in secret, all undeclared, though that is demanded by the U.S. Constitution rendering every one of these wars to have been illegal under our Constitution.

The United States military now has 170 publicly known bases and operations scattered around the world and many more secret ones, some of which have only recently been identified. The U.S. still has troops from World War II stationed across Europe and Asia, and over 30,000 soldiers remain in Korea, from a conflict which ended in 1954.

We finally have a President who is questioning these things and trying to bring peace to the Korean Peninsula and elsewhere, realizing that it is these often fabricated conflicts that may be good for the war industry but have drained our treasury. Donald Trump has also been the first president in my life who understands that you don't beat a bully by appeasing him. You kick his ass—or at least show that you can or are willing to do so—and the rest generally takes care of itself.

Let's Talk Openly About The Greatest Threat

Even the Middle East is being calmed by the President's bold approach, and appears to be achieving historic peace—again through strength rather than appeasement. His first triumph—bringing the more moderate nations of Islam together against the most violent, was brilliant. Then, President Trump moved the U.S. Embassy from Tel Aviv to Jerusalem, making it clear where he stood, but also making him the first president in almost three decades of promises to actually keep his word.

That will inevitably strengthen Israel against those whose ideology as written by their 'prophet' demands that there can be no peace until "All Christians, Jews, and Kaffirs [Non-Believers]," have either been subdued (enslaved) or "killed, crucified, limbs on either side cut off"...well, you get the picture. Those are the actual written words of Mohammed himself, so if you are offended by what they say, take it up with a mullah or cleric rather than me, but this is what 1/7 of the world now follows as a belief system, and it is not elective. Jihad is mandatory and if a follower is unwilling to do these things, then they are to be "killed, crucified, limbs on either side cut off" by their neighbours as punishment.

No wonder they all want to move to Europe and America.

The problem is that people who hold this as a "religion"—this foreign belief system that requires the murder of everyone who disagrees with them until the host nation is subdued, and then subjecting it to Sharia Law which requires these atrocities—well, that's the problem in itself. They bring this violent political ideology with them and are required, once their numbers are sufficient, to implement it on their host society. Take a look at London. There are muslim settlements there now where the Chief Constable is required to have those he hires as police to be approved by the mullah and they have their own Sharia courts.

Regardless of what muslims may tell you about their 'religion of peace, (as President Barack Hussein Obama once called it) that is what they are required to do—and they will. Why? Because that is also from the Quran. Deceit in this process is not only consecrated by the prophet, but was practiced by him when alive and recommended as the means for future followers to secretly move in and take new lands. Mohammed did it himself in Medina. You might just want to look at France, Sweden or England of today, as example, or even take a day trip to Dearborn, Michigan.

And as a muslim, if you do not adhere to those words—according to their prophet, not me—then they cannot be a 'good' muslim, and are to have these same atrocities perpetrated on themselves by their truly 'good' muslim neighbors who will dismember them.

I read not only the Quran but the Hadiths after hearing congressional testimony from retired four-star Admiral James "Ace" Lyons. He informed Congress, *"Islam is not a religion. It is a political ideology of world-domination through murder and mayhem"*— and went on in a lengthy speech detailing how every president since Jimmy Carter has been too weak to recognize what Islam truly is. Admiral Lyons further warned that it is not to be appeased or allowed to gain strength in one's nation *"without dire consequences."*[1]

So these are not my words or 'hate speech.' This is a very dangerous belief system that has consequences for any who allow it to take root in their nation—by the order of their prophet, who claims to have been the one and final messenger of Allah—the moon god of ancient Arabia.[2] When muslims repeat, "there is no god but Allah, and Mohammed is his messenger," they are not talking about yours.

I highly recommend that you read, *"The Story of Mohammed: Islam unveiled,"* by British author Harry Richardson, who painstakingly put the writings of Mohammed in sequence, from his humble beginnings in Mecca trying to unsuccessfully start his cult along the designs of Jesus Christ (his writings actually begin with the story of Jesus and his mother

---

[1] https://www.liveleak.com/view?t=faa_1457147943

[2] "In ancient Arab the Allah was considered to be the supreme God/deity (as Moon-God) and Arab Pagans worshipped Allah before Islam arrived." http://faithfreedom.org/Articles/skm30804.htm

Mary as the base, who Mohammed claims to have been his predecessor 'prophet'), to the dangerous, murdering, raping raider, warlord and slave-trader he became in his later years taking entire tribes and regions by force and pillage.

The Hadiths (the gospels of Islam) brag of Mohammed cutting off the heads of 800 Jews in just two days—after they had kindly sustained him and his troops for a year—raping the wife of their leader, making her his sex slave after murdering her father, brothers and husband and selling her children into slavery. This in Islam is 'the perfect man' and these stories are told young men proudly by clerics and mullahs as an example of how they are to be. Jihad, you will learn in Richardson's book (and Mohammed's own words), is not a choice, but a mandate, and it can never end until all 'non-believers' are murdered or enslaved through violence and deceit.

It is estimated that 70% of Islam's followers are illiterate, so they cannot be held to account for their ignorance of what is said in the book by the man they die for to spread his ideology, but that also makes them (and this ideology) more lethal. When young men are taught by their highest authorities that death in the name of 'jihad' against any non-muslims is their only way from dire poverty directly to heaven—where scores of fresh virgins await them—is it really surprising that they are so happy to die?

The Hadith written by Mohammed's last wife, Aisha, tells in her own words how she was forced to marry the warlord at the age of six. Women, under Islam, are a man's 'tilth' in the self-proclaimed prophet's commands, which is an old word for property. A father literally gives ownership of his daughter to her husband. If he dies, she becomes the property of his brother, and so on. Women must be owned by a man.

President Trump has done his homework on this topic far better than the feminists, it appears. He realizes that only through overwhelming strength and alliances with the moderate Middle Eastern leaders who publicly cling to this backward ideology of violence only out of lack of choice, can be trusted to move forward toward peace. The Mullahs and Clerics of Iran are not among them, and will never forego violence and murder, or set their women free, until their own deaths or downfall.

Peace on the Korean Peninsula

As I write this, a summit has also been set to end the Korean conflict where U.S. forces lost over 2,000 planes and five battleships, with over two million casualties and deaths on both sides, but "war" was never declared. It is my fervent hope and belief that this businessman-President will continue ending long-standing conflicts through strength during his tenure so we can bring Johnny home.

The Constitution allows for our Navy to be outfitted and maintained at all times to keep the seas and our borders safe. The powerful air support they carry on their decks also fall within those limits—but sending our sons and daughters to fight wars on the ground of foreign nations requires a vote of Congress. A century of Progressive leaders have spent our revenues destroying others to enrich the war industry, its suppliers, and satisfy political donors, while our infrastructure crumbles. That is not only stupid, it is unconstitutional. Our forces are to be defensive in nature, not offensive, and I think we have a man in the White House that gets that—while seeing our enemies for who they really are, rather than being naive and trying to appease them or think they can be changed.

The most conservative comparison of U.S. military spending to the rest of the world I can find (The Economist, 02/19/2011, p. 14) places it *"currently equivalent to that of the next 20 countries combined."*

Even the most ardent hawk must see that such wasteful spending and excessive pandering to the military-industrial complex has little, if anything, to do with *defense*. The only beneficiaries of war are those who supply it and finance it. Those are the same entities and corporations that now control our representatives in Congress or this could not have happened. When is enough, enough?

The nation's first president, George Washington, warned in his Farewell Address to stay out of foreign affairs and instead, *"Observe good faith and justice towards all nations; cultivate peace and harmony with all."* Our leaders have refused George Washington's advice and stay in a state of perpetual war. As James Madison pointed out, *"No nation could preserve its freedom in the midst of continual warfare,"* and we have not.

The United States, under Progressive and corporate control, has caused this. It is time to get back to the basics of the Founders' intent.

So What Would a Legal Military Look Like?

The proper and only role of the American military is as a defensive force, *in time of declared war.* The only national force authorized to exist in times of peace is the United States Navy, which is designated to protect the nation's coasts and keep sea lanes open for commercial traffic. Article I, Section 8 is clear. Federal government is *"To provide and maintain a Navy,"* but that is our only external force during times of peace.

In time of declared war—and only then—Congress is authorized *"To raise and support Armies, but no Appropriation of Money to that Use shall be for a longer Term than two years."*

A standing federal army, when no war has been declared, was and is un-constitutional, plain and simple. One can be raised in time of declared war, but no standing army is allowed in time of peace, other than State Militias. That does not mean that the nation was to be defenseless. Our Founders styled their military land forces after the most successful defense force in human history, the Swiss Army.

Why? Because the Swiss model had already kept that nation out of war for hundreds of years in the 1770s and 1780s when Madison, Washington and Jefferson were planning our military, and it has ever since. That is still our nation's model by law and constitution, and the means by which George Washington was able to defeat the greatest army on earth during the Revolutionary War.

The Swiss Army has successfully defended its nation since the 1500s, despite Europe being a battlefield all around it for most of that period of history. The Swiss Confederation successfully maintained its neutrality and peace for half a millennia, and has the highest per capita standard of living in the world because of it. *"War is the parent of armies; from these proceed debt and taxes…,"* as James Madison warned.

Swiss leadership is under a triumvirate, as Benjamin Franklin wanted for the United States presidency. The Swiss have not squandered their nation's wealth on war as U.S. presidents have squandered ours. "Progressive" U.S. leaders left the constitutional Swiss model over a century ago, and have since bankrupted the nation with their standing army and continuous warfare.

The expenditures wasted on corporate-sponsored war for the past fiscal *year* would have funded a *constitutional* military for most, if not all, of our nation's history.

A *constitutional* army is very inexpensive and has but one purpose, which is to protect and preserve the independence of the nation. The Swiss model on which our Founders based our own was and is based on a system of universal cantonal conscription under which every Swiss male is expected to serve as a member of his Canton's (State) military between 20 and 42 years of age. Officers serve until the age of 52. This is the *constitutional* method of State militias as described in Article I, Section 8.

Initial training is followed by 10 three-week refresher courses. Swiss females also serve on a volunteer basis in the women's military force. The nation's people are its army.

Swiss soldiers keep their weapons, ammunition and equipment in their homes and are ready to deploy at a moment's notice. Gunnery practice is obligatory each year and it is performed in civilian clothes.

This model of military develops and maintains an extraordinary degree of trust between government and its citizens *as it was designed to do.* In our model, the States were to control the land forces for their protection (internal) and the federal government was to control the navy to protect the coast (external) and sea lanes. That is still our *constitutional military model,* and it is not too late to return to it.

A federal government whose army is its own private citizenry under State or cantonal controlled military units, cannot abuse them or violate that trust except at its own peril. It also cannot subject them to the tyranny of Progressive and corporate interests to their own detriment as our federal government has done now for over a century, which also seems to be the only logical explanation for the United States government to have so flagrantly violated the U.S. Constitution and created its standing armies.

So How Can We Fix This, While Cleaning Up The Prog's Messes?

Progressive corporate interests starting with J.P. Morgan, need aggressive mercenary assault forces, not defensive ones. The resulting military-industrial complex wants perpetual war-for-profit and that is what they got, thanks to their ability to purchase the representatives of *We the People.*

The last time the United States of America was attacked by a foreign nation was in 1812 and a constitutional American army defeated them, the British Army, the most powerful in the world, so soundly that neither they nor anyone else has ever tried since.

As the Swiss and United States have proven, no standing army of mercenaries is a match for well-trained citizen-warriors protecting their homes and families.

No army wants to go door-to-door against the Swiss and none has ever tried, including Napoleon or Hitler, though they controlled all the nations around them. Trained citizen-warriors defending their homes are worth ten conscripted soldiers. Even the brief Swiss alliance of its French-speaking cantons with Napoleon was not a war, and lasted only briefly.[3]

The camaraderie and sense of community built by regional defense forces are anathema to Progressivism and strong central government. They do not serve corporate America either, which is why Progs created an unconstitutional federal standing army to replace them, in my opinion. It is time for this constitutional anomaly to end before it destroys our nation. Let the corporations hire their own army.

The land forces must revert to State-controlled and managed military units, to be called upon by federal government, only in time of a defensive war, officially declared by Congress.

Military bases and National Guard posts located in each State could easily revert to local control and scale down to be defensive in nature rather than offensive as they are today. If anything, local soldiers, living at their homes in that State, ready to defend it or the nation, is a far greater *defense and deterrent* to outside hostilities than any other, while causing no hatred abroad.

---

[3] *The French-speaking cantons of the Swiss confederation were lured into an alliance with Napoleon in 1798 and created the Helvetic Republic. By 1803, they rejoined the Republic to make the original 13 cantons. Six new cantons later joined to form the 19 canton Helvetic Confederation as it exists today*

Any needed foreign intelligence would be the responsibility of the United States Navy, the nation's external force. A nation engaging in *"Peace, commerce, and honest friendship with all nations — entangling alliances with none,"* as Thomas Jefferson advocated, has no need of further intelligence capabilities or a standing army, once we extricate ourselves from the quagmire left the President by lesser men before him.

How others choose to live is their own affair unless they encroach on our soil or our people, which is very unlikely in a peaceful nation that minds its own business as the Swiss have proven for half a millennia. Should any nation make such a terrible mistake as to attack them (or us), they would think they stepped into a hornet's nest.

All military power (external) must revert to the control of the U.S. Congress. Internal and land-based forces must return to the control of the States. The U.S. President has no authority over either except in time of declared war, at which time he becomes Commander and Chief for the duration of the conflict only.

Americans must honestly ask themselves whom war really serves. War does not serve the young men and women who die in them before they've had an opportunity to taste life. It does not serve their parents and loved ones who lose them, and in fact, it does them great harm.

Invading foreign nations, even with good intentions, is rarely a service in the long run. It is not our place, constitutionally, to force our way of life on anyone at the point of a gun anyway, though good intentions have rarely had anything to do with invasions by the United States, once the truth became known. Recent wars served other interests.

* * *

Stop the Lies and You Stop the Wars

America's current wars like those of the past century of wars were sold to the nation with lies. Public sentiment was played upon by politicians and hyped by the corporate media. In the end, the only beneficiaries were the suppliers of war toys and services; and the bankers who financed them.

Six hundred thousand Iraqis died at our nation's hands to extricate the puppet, Saddam Hussein, whom our own government's CIA put in place there years ago. Former CIA Director and President of the United States, George H.W. Bush, used to refer to his CIA asset in Iraq, Saddam Hussein (as well as Bush's CIA operative, Panamanian strongman, Manuel Noriega, whom Bush also overthrew) as 'my boy.' And that they both were. He turned them, he used them, and then they were imprisoned or killed.

The infrastructure of the Iraqi nation, thanks to Daddy Bush and Junior, has been obliterated and over one of every forty of its people is now dead. We sowed those seeds 50 years ago, and we are still reaping the sadness of them—as are the Iraqi people—today.

Forty percent of the soldiers sent by our nation's politicians to fight that war are returning home with mental problems, which is only natural. No sane person can be told to invade and murder innocent people and destroy their country without having psychological difficulties from so doing, or be psychotic to the point that it has no effect on them.

The United States Constitution does not allow this kind of activity and it must stop now. Foreign bases must close, except those necessary to keep the nation's navy repaired and fueled. No nation has need of 170+ bases around the world, with troops ready to invade foreign lands, if it is a free and peaceful country as ours was meant to be.

Those young men and women need to help rebuild our own nation; a constitutional America. It's time to bring Johnny (and Jane) home.

Action Plan

Congress must reassert its authority over the military forces and and either declare our present military actions as 'wars' giving the President authority as Commander and Chief, or end them. There is no constitutional in-between.

Federal land-based forces must devolve to State control as required by the United States Constitution. Congress may prescribe their training regimen and call them to service in time of declared war, but they are the responsibility, and under the control of, the respective States between those declared wars.

Foreign U.S. military presence—other than is necessary to keep sea lanes open for commercial traffic and gather intelligence under the U.S. Navy —needs to be wound down and come to an end once our nation's interests are secured. No more wars to promote the interests of Progressive donors, corporations and bankers—or to drain our nation's treasury.

Chapter 11

PUTTING THE CORPORATE GENIE BACK IN THE BOTTLE

THE common denominator of our national ills from uncontrollable pollution and unnecessary wars, to bloated federal government and our loss of freedom, can be traced to the Progressive-dominated corporate powers that control the United States federal government—and most others—today. I am not discussing the small companies that provide most of the nation's jobs, but the international giants and cartels that have flourished under the unconstitutional curse known as "Progressivism."

International corporations are now the dominant cultural and economic force on earth and directly or indirectly control the planet's stores of natural resources. The transnational corporate giants hold combined assets valued at more than the total worth of over half the nations of the world. They also control most of its governments, directly or indirectly, and write most of those nations' legislation and laws. This has acted to neutralize national governments as a safeguard against abuses by international corporations and cartels, or to effectively punish their misdeeds.

Big corporations survive and thrive only in an environment of big governments and world powers. Theirs is a symbiotic relationship.

The huge sums of money these corporations dangle before politicians the world over in such dizzying amounts would tempt the most chaste and honest of men. Those are characteristics rarely associated with politicians and to that temptation, they have proven themselves quite vulnerable.

Legislation is bought and sold as if in a market (perhaps 'brothel' is a better analogy) and the loser is always *We the People*. This prostitution of power and money must come to an end.

While some call this the exercise of free speech, it's not. It is bribery.

Capitalism? Not Hardly

Adam Smith, the father of capitalist theory according to most economists, is the man many of these huge corporate entities would no doubt consider as their patron saint. What these oligarchs practice, however, is as far from Smith's capitalism as its opposing economic theories, such as communism. Adam Smith warned of this back in 1776 and described corporations and "joint stock companies" as they were commonly called in his day, "nuisances in every respect."[1] Smith claimed that they "have in the long run proved, universally, either burdensome or useless, and have either mismanaged or confined the trade."[2] Smith wrote:

> *"The usual corporate spirit, wherever the law does not restrain it, prevails in all regulated companies. When they have been allowed to act according to their own natural genius, they have always, in order to confine the competition to as small a number as possible, endeavoured to subject the trade to many burdensome regulations."*[3]

---

[1] *Smith, Adam. An Inquiry into the Nature and Causes of the Wealth of Nations. Vol. 36, Chronology of Great Authors, Encyclopaedia Brittanica Inc., Chicago, IL, Sixth Edition, 1996, p.313*
[2] *Ibid.*
[3] *Ibid.*

This process of kicking away the ladder after climbing to the top unrestrained, has worked well for large American corporations and professions such as law and medicine. *"Burdensome regulations"* only benefit those already well-established in the industry or profession, by making entry of new competitors increasingly difficult if not impossible, thereby protecting those already in it from true capitalism and competition. Big corporate interests need big government to employ the law to protect them from competition by would-be entrants into the industry so they seek to limit entry. Regulation and red-tape worked in Adam Smith's day, and they do today, keeping small companies out of the marketplace, and professions such as medicine and law, limited in numbers, by their own private monopolies.

Once again, we finally have a businessman in the White House who understands this and has mandated that two job-killing Progressive rules inflicted on the nation be stricken down for every new one imposed. The Trump Administration has far exceeded that promise by striking down 22 regulations for every new one, which is rapidly removing the shackles for the people who matter—American businessmen and women who will be free to innovate and prosper, while hiring their fellow citizens. Adam Smith described the corporate power over the law-making process as *"like an overgrown standing army, they have become formidable to the government and upon many occasions intimidate the legislature."*[4]

Those legislators who support every proposal for the corporate interests and monopolists, Smith stated enjoy *"great popularity and influence with an order of men whose numbers and wealth render them of great importance."* Of those who oppose them, Adam Smith wrote *"neither the highest rank, nor the greatest public services can protect him from the most infamous abuse and detraction, from personal insults, nor sometimes from real danger, arising from the insolent outrage of furious and disappointed monopolists."*[5]

---

[4] *Ibid.*
[5] *Ibid.*

This often named 'father of capitalism' was relentless in his attacks on these market distorting anomalies known as "corporations" and "joint-stock companies." He listed 55 of their failures from his day in *The Wealth of Nations*, to make his point. Perhaps Smith's greatest insult was when he wrote, "*they are certainly altogether useless. To be merely useless is perhaps the highest eulogy which could ever justly be bestowed upon a regulated company.*"[6]

The History of Corporations in America

Big corporate America would be far better suited with Genghis Khan or Attila the Hun as its patron saint rather than Adam Smith. Companies were his sworn enemy, and what they do today in America is not Adam Smith's capitalism, it is Progressive government-sanctioned oligarchy. From the Virginia Company land corporation, which established the colony in Jamestown in 1606, and the Plymouth Company (also chartered in 1606) destined for Massachusetts, the corporate virus was transplanted to America. It has gone from a mere nuisance like a common cold, to life threatening in its virulent present-day form.

Once the Constitution was established as law of the land in America, corporate charters were granted, but only for purposes that could be claimed to be in some public interest or service. That system worked well for much of our history. Charters were granted to corporations for expanding ports, building bridges, as example, and importing certain goods that were needed but not available or produced in America. Public service had to be a component of a corporation's reason for being and these charters were granted for a fixed-time only.

The canal-building era, which began in 1817 when the State of New York chartered a privately-owned corporation to build the 363 mile Erie Canal

---

[6] *Ibid.*

between Lake Erie and the Hudson River, was a turning point. Such public service corporations were chartered then for as few as ten years, and only while they performed the service for which they were created. The corporation and its charter then expired, and any remaining business became a non-corporate proprietorship, without any special protections or privileges from government.

This was the marketplace where Adam Smith's theories that people *"are led by an invisible hand to make nearly the same distribution of the necessaries of life,"* and true capitalism thrived and actually benefited the public as well as the proprietor. All corporations in our nation's early history were held to such standards. No State would authorize one to exist unless it served a public need and corporations were not allowed to buy one another or keep monopolistic powers.

Failure to fulfill their purpose, or to carry out the proposed public service or fiduciary duty, was also a cause for charter revocation.

This system survived for roughly a century before the advent of the Golden Era of the Robber Barons of the railroads, which changed it forever. Private corporations were given land grants of over 130 million acres from the humble beginnings of the Baltimore and Ohio Railroad in 1830 up through the completion of the transcontinental line in 1869 when the Central Pacific connected to the Union Pacific in Promontory, Utah. These government grants were the foundations of the vast Progressive fortunes which would soon take control of the nation's political process.

From Andrew Carnegie's first fortune earned selling railroad bonds, through the oligarchs Cornelius Vanderbilt (New York Central Railroad), James Hill (Northern Pacific), Leland Stanford (Central Pacific), E. Henry Harriman (Union Pacific), Collis Huntington (Southern Pacific), and on to J.P. Morgan himself, the die was cast.

The crowning blow of granting citizenship to these bodiless entities in 1886 (*Santa Clara County v. Southern Pacific Railroad*), gave these government-subsidized millionaires the means to buy control of the nation, with fortunes granted them by government through their *public service* monopolies.

A Tale Stranger Than Fiction

So how did this granting of unnamed powers to the corporate masters of America ever come about? It did not begin with *Citizens United* in 2010, as many think, or even the 5 of 9 imaginative SCOTUS "interpreters" currently sitting on the bench who voted in its favor. It began long, long ago, based on an offhand comment by Chief Justice Morrison Waite in the year 1886, *before* the case *Santa Clara County v. Southern Pacific Railroad Co.* even began.

Judge Waite's pre-case comment also had nothing to do with the notion of corporate citizenship or the case itself. Santa Clara was a tax case, but his comment was later added to the Notes at the request of the Court Reporter. So who was this Court Reporter, J.C. Bancroft Davis, and why did he want to add a topic that was not even part of the case in its record?

More surprising than making law out of a court reporter's notes of offhand comments, however, is that this particular scribe, J.C. Bancroft Davis, was the former president of Newburgh and New York Railway. Davis—a potential beneficiary of his own "interpretation"—and was somehow planted in this case as the Court Reporter.

It would be like Chief Justice Roberts allowing Jeff Bezos to be Court Reporter while the Supremes were dealing with a case regarding taxation of on-line commerce, to put it in modern context—and his adding notes

— that became law —regarding net neutrality, when that was not a topic before the court or in its decision.

As you are probably seeing now from history, when the Progressives want something to happen, law is a small matter. Stacking the deck is what they do—for their "higher purpose" of course—which is to (benevolently) control us. But let's not forget that their 'benevolent' control has brought us into roughly 180 wars since the last one that was legally declared (World War II), costing the lives of hundreds of thousands of our children, while these same Progressives have used ungranted powers and fabricated 314,000 laws outside of their authority, to disenfranchise and/or imprison one-fourth of us. If that is 'benevolence', my fellow citizens, we can do without it.

But how did they take us over and no one was able to catch them or stop them? No plausible explanation has ever been offered as to how a president of an associated railroad was allowed to become the Court Reporter of the United States Supreme Court in a case that so greatly affected him and his fellow barons (and us), but it is an historical fact. I urge you to look it up for yourself.

And as if to prove it was a contrived scheme, Railroad Exec *cum* Supreme Court Reporter, Davis added his commentary *after* the decision was rendered on the tax issue, so subsequent courts could "interpret" his Notes as law or *stare decisis*, though corporate citizenship was never an issue in the case, nor any part of the decided facts. And none of J.P. Morgan-controlled newspapers—26 of them— reported the crime, only that the court had ruled that corporations were citizens.

Chief Justice Morrison Waite specifically wrote to Davis, "*I leave it with you to determine whether anything need be said about it [the comment] in the report inasmuch as we avoided meeting the constitutional question in the decision.*"

This was in response to Railroad Executive Davis's specific request in writing to Chief Justice Waite seeking approval to insert pre-planned comments about 'corporate citizenship' into the record. In service to J. P. Morgan and the railroad barons, Waite did it.

How could anyone possibly make up a story so bizarre? It is history, and part of the official Supreme Court record of the case—just like Progressive Secretary of State, Philander Knox's, faking of the Sixteenth Amendment's passage was admitted by the Supreme Court in *U.S. v. Thomas*—but no one in the press has talked about it, and no one in government ever corrected it.

To put it in modern context—it's like CNN missing the spying on the Trump campaign and takedown of a sitting president by every member of the Obama Progressive cabal still buried in government—and no one saying a damn word—which is exactly what they have done—so maybe some things never change.

But when I read *Santa Clara* and realized who this 'clerk' really was—even after seeing all the other misdeeds of the Progressives of yesterday and today—this sin was beyond imagination.

Based on this thinnest of commentary by a conflicted court reporter (and seemingly planted by Progs, given the circumstances) corporate America inundated SCOTUS almost every year thereafter for decades based on this imaginary right as "citizens" culminating with *Citizens United v. FEC* in 2010 (and other decisions since). The "interpreters" in black robes went along with the fiction claiming it was accepted by their predecessors, and it is now cemented into 'decided law.' We, the shareholders in our social contract with Government, have lost our country in a hostile takeover.

Time For a New Sheriff

America's major corporations now have the keys to our nation. They were handed them by nine "interpreters" in black robes charged with protecting our Constitution who have completely ignored it, while acting in violation of it, as it was not their purview to add fictitious parties to the contract, simply to enforce it.

But how can we punish the majority of the Supreme Court when they make up laws or refuse to follow the Constitution they swore to uphold?

We can't, which is why my seemingly mad idea of putting Constitutional advocates and historians on the Supreme Court instead of 'Progressive' lawyers privately committed to destroying it, might not seem like such a bad or crazy idea now.

We the People were robbed of our birthright like the settlers in the old Western movies of my youth were when they got in the way of these same Robber Barons by just being there. The Sheriff was bought off by the rich guy (see in your mind, George Soros, with an evil-looking moustache and black cowboy hat) and their lands were stolen from them, like we have had our nation taken from us. The difference is, we haven't had a tall, dusky stranger on the horizon riding in with a sixgun on his hip to save us like in the old movies—until now.

We the People were on our own against the Progressives and their gangsters of council and court for the longest time, but just maybe.....there is finally a new Sheriff in town (see in your mind Donald Trump, clean-shaven, in a white cowboy hat) willing to give them that hard look of his at high noon— and make them blink.

* * *

The Rest of the Story

Once corporations were legally able to bribe politicians using their status as "citizens" after the unconstitutional decision in *Santa Clara County*, the United States government became a tool in their service rather than a limiting or restraining factor on them, just as Abraham Lincoln predicted.

Big corporations and big "Progressive" government were soul mates. They thrived together, sucking the nation and its people dry, while creating the great disparity we see today between rich and poor; powerful and powerless today.

The United States went from the freest, most prosperous nation on earth, to a bankrupt police state owing $75 trillion, which it can never repay. $54 trillion of that debt (borrowed from Social Security) is to *We the People*, but it is unlikely we will ever see it. The rest is owed largely to foreign nations and banks, and is growing at nearly $2 trillion each year as the Progressives dig us ever deeper into insolvency and tyranny.

The question is not whether to stop them or not, but whether or not there is time left to do so. Between their continued stripping of our planet of all its natural resources, and their constant wars to secure them, we simply may not survive long enough to break their iron grip on our nation, its politicians, or our world. And that is why we should embrace Trump. He is not controlled by them, certainly not by the press, and dislikes them almost as much as they hate him.

The first step is to wrest control of Congress from the corporations as laid out in the Chapter Two, but more must be done to break their means of ever controlling our nation again.

It was not until the States of New Jersey and Delaware were coerced into relaxing their laws regarding corporations at the behest (and cash) of John D. Rockefeller and J.P. Morgan that the corporate genie was completely out of the bottle, so this seems like the place to start putting him back.

These *enabling acts* as they were known, were sold to the States as means of generating revenues. Once adopted by Delaware and New Jersey, the race to the bottom was on. Other States quickly followed suit and corporations were given incredible power and rights, while being concurrently relieved of any attendant responsibilities to the public.

Public service was no longer required and true ownership could be occluded from view in some States, as is still the case in Delaware and Nevada today. Freed of public service requirements, and protected by the corporate veil of liability, the nation was the corporations' oyster. Politicians have been bought and sold like livestock to do their bidding ever since.

So Here's How We Fix It

Corporations are still formed and regulated at the State level and they should be limited once more in their use, scope and boundaries. Each State should prescribe, by law, what it demands of any corporation, be it one of their own or from another state or nation, before it can operate (or continue to operate) within that State. There should once again be a requirement of public service and need, otherwise, businesses should remain proprietorships or limited affairs, which would keep them on a human scale, unable to control governments and the political process.

There will be court battles and lawsuits aplenty, and it will not be an easy task, but the States must re-assert their power to control what goes on in their sovereign jurisdictions, if nothing else, to break the hegemony of the national and transnational corporations over this nation, if not the world.

Corporations have no sovereignty. Nothing in the United States Constitution justifies the outrageous decision in *Santa Clara County v. Southern Pacific Railroad* granting citizenship rights to a box of papers and a corporate seal back in 1886. The history of how these oligarchs contrived this Supreme Court decision—which you now know— should itself be cause for its overturn, as well as all of the subsequent decisions based on it. There simply is no legal basis for corporate citizenship, period. The word *corporation* is not mentioned in the United States Constitution, and that contract is with *We the People, not Them the Corporations.*

American jurisprudence holds that an unconstitutional statute or judicial decision, though having the name and form of law, is wholly void and ineffective for any purpose.

The Supreme Court cannot (legally) create words that are not in the U.S. Constitution, nor can it confer rights not authorized by it. The day of corporate rule over the United States (and its High Court) must draw to a close soon or our nation is lost to them forever.

This effort can begin at the State level by re-establishing the principles upon which corporations were originally allowed to be formed—public service. Unless a public service can be established and fulfilled by that corporation, and that State's criterion for formation can be met, the corporation should face dissolution and be returned to a proprietorship of owners, or be barred from operation within that State's boundaries.

State law and requirements of resident ownership or board control should also be applied to any corporation doing business within the State, as they once were, ending the hegemony of a handful of retail, banking, and corporate giants. This would, simultaneously, act to restore local trade, local manufacturers, local retailers, and local suppliers.

Capital would once more remain in the State and local banks and communities to fund and finance regional industries and diverse projects of local need and small businesses, rather than shifting to and pooling in the corporate capitals of the world to fund transnational operations elsewhere.

Local entrepreneurs, small business, and regional banks, could again fluoresce and build real, interdependent communities, putting an end to one-mill towns that dry up when the non-resident owners find cheaper labor elsewhere. The big-box stores, brands and chains, which do not serve any real public function, could be required to divest to local ownership or be replaced with a flourishing local economy of trade and commerce by individual proprietorships. Local products, foods, and supplies would supplant the foreign made and grown, and revenues would remain within the community.

Business ownership and control over our lives and our communities would return to a human, local scale and scope, ending the rule of the corporate oligarchs from afar.

Non-resident corporate giants could no longer soil our rivers, lakes, shores and earth, protected by politicians from Washington, while leaving their mess and poisons behind them when they pull up stakes and slip away in the middle of the night for those who live there to suffer and repair.

A restored sense of community and common purpose would settle upon the land, as was once the case in America. The rich and diverse patchwork of regional cultures and life-styles that once existed could again revive and flourish.

This is not utopic thinking or dreaming, it is how it once was in America. In the years before the corporate takeover of the nation, foreign visitors such as the eloquent Alexis de Tocqueville, were amazed by what they saw.[7] He wrote of people living lives of such vitality in extraordinary freedom and peace that was unknown in Europe. Life with no masters or monarchs where man existed in an egalitarian society of unadulterated liberty was something so foreign to the rest of what de Tocqueville called the "*modern world*", that it was looked on with wonder and envy by the masses, and feared by the rulers and oligarchs in Europe.

There is no question that there were horrible injustices and unforgivable wrongs done by the rich and powerful in that day as well. The scourge of slavery in parts of the nation and mistreatment of those forced into that foul institution by federal government and the oligarchs of that day will be a perpetual stain on the nation's honor and psyche. Federal government both instituted and allowed these horrible circumstances, but it also had a hand in its undoing. Correcting injustices is a valid duty of federal government. Instituting them is not.

The 130 million acres federal government gave away to the Robber Barons of the 1800s were each stolen by that same federal government from the indigenous people who had lived on this land for what we now know

---

[7] *As recorded in de Tocqueville's classic, Democracy in America*

to have been tens of thousands of years. In fact, the whole nation was pilfered from these people who had built their own societies of amazing grandeur before Hernando DeSoto and the swine that accompanied him in 1539, delivered the poxes that would decimate them.

There is no way to adequately recompense the Africans who labored under slavery to build the nation, or the native Americans whose lands were stolen and upon which it was built, except by creating a fair and free society wherein all of their descendants can again flourish and prosper.

The concepts of human freedom and egalitarianism were not brought to these shores by the European invaders. They were found here upon their arrival. The Founders marveled in their writings at the proud American Indian who knew no master and followed no leader except by his own choice. What Rousseau and Locke wrote about had been a way of life for centuries in America, but was yet unknown in most of Europe.

Returning to a just and free society where no man (or corporation) controls another, would be a small but due token to both the African American and the Native American.

From the Virginia Company, which murdered the Powhatans who had saved the Jamestown colonists, through the railroad corporations that bribed the federal government to steal the natives' lands by force of arms, the corporations were second only to smallpox as the Indian's worst and fiercest enemy.

From the federally-sanctioned slave importation monopolies of the 1700s to the federal protection of strike-busters in service to Andrew Carnegie under color of law, the African-American and all oppressed parts of society can hail corporate America as their foe and a great—if not greatest — source of their misery.

Progressive corporate power now controls both of our nation's political parties, leaving little hope for change unless they can no longer fund candidates, as suggested in Chapter Three. Our First Founding Father, George Washington, warned against these "parties" and loyalty to them rather than the nation. In his *Farewell Address*, Washington said that while parties may serve well *"in governments of a monarchical cast,"* by encouraging the spirit of liberty, *"in governments purely elective, it is a spirit not to be encouraged."*

Corporations have bribed their way out of the requirement of public servitude, taken control of our political parties, and shed all responsibilities to the public. The huge corporations are no longer just "useless" and a "nuisance" as they were in the 1700s when Adam Smith wrote about them; they are now dangerous, virulent, and a threat to our nation's solvency and world stability.

This danger of transnational and mega-corporations controlling our own government and representatives, must be addressed forthwith as a prerequisite to finding our way back to a constitutional America.

Action Plan

Begin the corporate reformation at State government level by revamping rules of incorporation on a state-by-state basis. Return requirement of public service to the granting of public charters (for large stock issuing companies doing business across State borders), and make them for a fixed time, dependent upon continued service and good behavior in that State, or refuse renewal.

Establish strict rules by which any corporation must abide in order to be allowed to incorporate or operate within the State. Some suggestions might include:

1. Corporations cannot directly or indirectly make contributions of any kind to political candidates, forums, PACs or even political parties.

2. Corporations engaged in any potentially harmful activity which may damage environment must post a surety bond at maximum foreseeable cost of reparation, and shareholders must sign personal, non-waivable guarantees to cover any overage.

3. Corporations from other States with operations, outlets, offices or any presence within the State must comply with all State rules which should require local board members, management with authority to override non-local decision making, and some local ownership; or suffer closure. Local control must be re-asserted. Non-compliant corporations from other States and nations might choose to sell local operations or franchises to State residents, but their national hegemony needs to be broken. The concept of free and open trade between the States applied to merchandise, not matters of control and how they operated within those States.

Chapter 12

THE SUSTAINABLE WAY FORWARD

Hernando de Soto landed at present-day Tampa Bay, Florida in the year 1539. He wrote in his journal of a land filled with people and areas of civilization which could not fit another dwelling. He and his 600 men traveled up through the present-day Carolinas and Tennessee, then south and west to the Mississippi River. DeSoto described a settled country and peaceful people with a meticulously cultivated landscape, where man lived in unison with nature.

What de Soto did not know was that the swine, horses and soldiers comprising his expedition were delivering a death warrant to those settled, peaceful people. Recent estimates by researcher Charles C. Mann, in his 2005 book, 1491: *New Revelations of the Americas Before Columbus*, (Knopf Publishing, New York) place the death-toll of the indigenous people of North and Central America as high as 97% from these unknown European poxes and plagues (previously estimated at 92%). The invaders' immunity to these diseases had taken centuries to develop, but the natives in America, were defenseless against them. It was the most horrific die-off of human kind in known history.

The British invaders, just 70 years later, found an empty landscape, hardly populated, with entire villages intact but devoid of a living soul. All that remained of the great cultures that had existed for tens of thousands of years were a handful of native Americans with their deep respect for Mother Earth, upon whose back they lived lightly; and the fierce sense of independence and love of liberty with which they would infect the invaders, leading ultimately to the severance of their ties with England in 1776.

But like the corporations of today, the invaders took the good without any of the responsibility attending it. They accepted the freedom aspect of the native culture, without the deep commitment and attendant responsibility to care for Mother Earth which accompanied and supported that lifestyle. They plundered freely, without regard or responsibility to the Great Provider and care of the source, respectively.

The invaders' treatment of the land and nature were shocking to the natives and disgusting even to some of their own. Historian William Strickland wrote a first-hand account of what he witnessed in his *Journal of a Tour of the United States of America 1794-1795*, and described the settlors as having:

> *"an utter abhorrence for the works of creation that exist on the place where he unfortunately settles himself. In the first place he drives away or destroys the more humanized Savage the rightful proprietor of the soil; in the next place he thoughtlessly and rapaciously exterminates all living animals, that can afford profit, or maintenance to man, he then extirpates the woods that cloath and ornament the country, and that to any but himself would be of the greatest value, and finally he exhausts and wears out the soil, and with the devastation he has thus committed usually meets with his own ruin; for by this time he is reduced to his original poverty; and it is then left him only to sally forth and seek the frontiers, a new country which he may again devour....The day appears not too distant when America so lately an unbroken forest, will be worse supplied with timber than most of the old countries of Europe."*

(New York Historical Society (1971) Library of Congress No. 75-165767)[1]

This is a near-perfect description of the traits exhibited by many transnational CEOs of today. They have no loyalty to place or nation—and as a political necessity—I suggest a way that we can cement State power into the future by taming these rapacious corporations so the Progressive and international takeover can never be repeated.

So this chapter is not just a 'tip of the cap' to my native ancestry or to the sincere folks concerned with what is happening to our natural world, but a serious financial and ecological proposal, as you will see in just three more pages. Please stick with me.

Our way forward as a nation will require not only that corporations return to the requirements and responsibilities of public service, but that all Americans accept the responsibility toward our homeland and Mother Earth that attends this freedom to live as we wish, which is a local concern—and I have some ideas on how that can benefit them.

The corporations that now own or control most of our natural resources, are drawing out that which took millions of years to concentrate in the earth, at rates that will utterly deplete them if allowed to continue. We are borrowing that which belongs to future generations, not us, and it is a debt that we cannot repay. The interstate and multinational corporations that benefit from it to the detriment of local (State) societies *should* pay, however, and that is only fair.

The same elements are on this planet that were here a billion years ago, but no more. We're drinking the same fresh water, as example, as the dinosaurs did over 200 million years ago. It evaporated, became a cloud, and came back down again purified, but it is the same water in quantity as was here in the days of the Tyrannosaurus Rex.

---

[1]Quoted in *The Great Work: Our Way Into the Future,* by Thomas Berry Three Rivers Press, New York (1999)

A rethinking of our approach to these resources is now necessary. It is incumbent upon us to develop new ways of dealing with the natural wealth of this land and sharing it with its dwellers rather than the shareholders of non-resident corporations. The holding of all, or nearly all, of the natural resources of the land by that top .1% of the population, and 90% by multinational corporations, cannot be justified by any logic or right —other than that it was the stated interests of Progressives to control us —benevolently they claim—and they have done it by giving control to their ilk at the expense of *We the People*.

Acceptable human freedoms do not extend to corporate control of the means by which others must live or the natural resources of a local people. The current model of over-extraction to the benefit of a very few, and to the detriment of local inhabitants and future, is not a fair or sustainable model.

Economist Herman Daly (*Steady State Economics* (1977)) and other sustainable-living advocates have devised methods and market-mechanisms which our nation must seriously consider to correct the imbalances, once corporate control of our representatives in Washington, DC is broken, as the control of this process must be local.

That which man produces by his own labor is his without question, but the natural resources which must sustain us all can hardly be claimed by one small group and should never have been allowed under corporate ownership or control from the beginning. The market model that could be our nation's salvation was developed by Daly forty years ago and subjected to ridicule by other economists, but many scoff no more. His book is back in print.

Daly proposed that ores, oil and all sources of relatively non-renewable resources which must last mankind forever, should be priced *and* sold accordingly. This market price must include all costs, such as entropy, rarity, and cost to the environment (both of extraction and waste on the other end). This true-costing model was to be based on the long-term needs of the local people rather than the next quarterly profit statement of a multi-national corporation.

These commodities should then be subject to a bidding process over and above all true costs, and based on the long view of mankind— controlled only at the State level.

The extractors, processors, and owners of the property would all be properly and profitably compensated for their part in the commodities' site ownership, removal and preparation but limits based on estimated remaining resources might be imposed on annual rates of extraction to protect future generations and their rights to those resources, again, by the States themselves—not federal government.

This is actually the model being used in Alaska today to a certain extent. The people of the State enjoy the revenue from its resources, not just multi-national corporations who extract and mine them.

The resulting price of the commodities would start from a bid base that included *all real costs*, not just the temporal ones, and would be market driven—rather than a multinational's desire to boost next quarter's earnings.

Profits realized from the auctioning of these commodity contracts would accrue to the benefit of the state or nation as a whole, depending on to whom they belong—or differently put, whether they were on State or Federal property.

To protect those funds from being pillaged by politicians, the income from them and their specific uses must be explicit and inviolable. If politicians have the power to borrow, re-direct, or spend them, it will be all for naught and end up like Social Security, which the political class and Progs have plundered since inception. Not a penny remains.

The prices of these commodities, which include all costs, will spark the birth of a real effort to reclaim waste and recycle as well. The cost of recycling plastic that now covers a substantial area of our oceans (or re-combining their carbon and hydrogen atoms to use as fuel), will be more cost-effective than drilling and processing the oil from which that plastic was originally derived. The billions of tons of scrap metal will be more cost effective to reclaim than mining the remaining stores which belong to future generations. The entropy factor of our existence will be reduced to a survivable level.

That which is drawn from the land of our States will be to the benefit of those who live there and no one else—like Alaska's oil.

As water (mankind's most precious commodity) becomes ever more scarce or fouled, this true-value costing may be expanded to it as well, as suggested in the 1990's work of Tony Allan of King's College London, and more recently, by Dutch scientist, Arjen Hoekstra's work at the University of Twente.

For example, it is estimated that 1,857 gallons of water are required to produce one pound of beef (versus 469 gallons per pound of chicken) using corporate factory farm methods. If the true cost of that water was added into the cost of a steak (or the 634 gallons required for just one hamburger), buying patterns and the demand for such environmentally harmful products might plummet—as would the factory methods employed by most if not all interstate and multinational producers.

Free-range chickens and grass-fed beef from small farms use almost no water in comparison, and most of what is used, is 'redeposited' back on the land.

If this sounds ridiculous, please put it in the context of our rapidly depleting groundwater supply. The Cargill/ADM grain monopolies export billions of gallons of water belonging to *We the People* each year in their agricultural products, and at no extra cost to themselves or their profits

—while drawing down aquifers such as the Ogallala in America's bread-basket by 30 meters (100 feet) since the 1940s.

Paying the true costs, including their host State's water they are exporting, might allow third-world nations to become self-sufficient once again by growing their own locally-produced crops rather than being force-fed ADM and Cargill's subsidized products and seeds, which would also be a boom to the State's own people in the end.

A local farmer could compete if all *real* costs were charged to the interstate or transnational—and if the corporations could not buy off members of the legislature to subsidize or unfairly protect them from real competition by small businesses and farms of the State they were elected to serve.

This integral plan is political, yes, but it has many financial benefits.

These multinational exports are drawing the underwater aquifers of the many parts of the United States which took thousands of years to fill, to dangerously low levels.[2] Groundwater is dropping drastically to levels that are becoming difficult to extract. *We the People* lose on every pound of grain ADM & Cargill export, while control much of the world's food supply is a result of freebies they get from the States which allow them to operate without paying future (or even present) costs to the people and farmers who live there.

Small and Local Has Been Proven More Efficient

The grain monopolies' displacement of local farms and farmers through underpriced products due to direct government subsidies and less direct advantages, (such as using increasingly scarce water belonging to *We the*

---

[2] *May 20, 2013 (Reuters) – "Water levels in U.S. aquifers, the vast underground storage areas tapped for agriculture, energy and human consumption, between 2000 and 2008 dropped at a rate that was almost three times as great as any time during the 20th century, U.S. officials said on Monday."*

People), harms everyone. The big interstate or international factory corporate farm is the most destructive to the environment and the most inefficient in terms of food production, per acre. In an article by George Monbiot, *"The Small Farmer is the planet's best hope,"* in the Guardian Weekly (June 13, 2008), the facts pellucidly make the point:

> *"Although the rich world's governments won't hear it, the issue of whether or not the world will be fed is partly a function of ownership. This reflects an unexpected discovery, first made in 1962 by the Nobel economist Amartya Sen and since confirmed by dozens of studies. There is an inverse relationship between the size of farms and the amount of crops they produce per hectare. The smaller they are, the greater the yield. In some cases the difference is enormous. A recent study in Turkey, for example, found that farms of less than one hectare are 20 times as productive as farms of more than 10 hectares. Sen's observation has been tested in India, Pakistan, Nepal, Malaysia, Thailand, Java, the Philippines, Brazil, Columbia, and Paraguay. It appears to hold almost everywhere."*

By being forced to pay the true cost of production and eliminating the direct and indirect subsidies the food monopolies receive from our federal government, they could not compete with the family farms they displaced and put out of business over the past century. A resurgence of small, diverse, and more productive farming could occur, greatly increasing the nation (and world's) food security while encouraging local production once more.

This model of true cost calculation and payment to the real owners of the natural resources would also have a much needed dampening effect on the junk and consumer culture which feeds this drawing down on limited resources and unlimited growth of landfills. Sensible methods that benefit the citizens of the States themselves could be applied to all interstate and multinational corporate and industrially made products, while excluding local in-state producers.

A pair of jeans, for example, requires 2,900 gallons of water to produce. One cotton T-shirt, takes 766 gallons. By pricing products to include these real costs and making that a cost to be paid by interstate and international companies, gross consumerism would be paid by those who *spend, spend, spend* rather than by everyone, and should steer far more revenue to the local State economies and their producers.

Waste, the manufacturing of unneeded junk, and the production of environmentally destructive products, would be reduced overnight by true cost allocation—all to the benefit of local producers and citizens. A pool of serious money could accumulate to help those less advantaged of our citizens and to secure future resources of the nation for posterity. This is the sustainable way forward—with serious positive political and financial consequences for the people living in these places.

Empowering Local People Also Prevents Tyranny

If the local economy of the State is booming and its people are prospering by charging corporations from other States and nations to pay the true costs of being there, how would the federal government ever talk those States and their people into giving up such liberties and protections again, now that they know what happens when their States no longer control the federal government? They tried that once.

Just look at what happened after the Seventeenth Amendment. Within years of its passage, our nation was thrust into a deep depression and our manufacturing base began to erode to free-traders. If the States saw an incredible boom to their own economies and people by true allocation of costs to the interstate and multinationals once allowed to control them, it will not be allowed to happen again.

The States are the sovereign in terms of control, not the other way around. The Senate must be restored to its Constitutional function so the Progressives can never make DC the masters again.

Environment is Protected

Just think this through from an environmental point of view as well. No one wants a dirty world or to drink putrid water, but if true cost allocation was made for resources, junkyards would become the ore mines of the future and landfills the source of industrial raw materials, solving two problems at one time. New waste accumulation would be minimal and past waste would become profitable to recycle and reuse.

Technology *cannot* cure the fact that our planet's resources are finite. Technology *can* make their usage more efficient and effective, however, and political changes (back to the Constitution) can make them benefit the real citizens of this nation, rather than corporations.

Technology can harness unlimited power from sun, wind, tides to provide additional energy. New clean-coal technology (*Coal Star*™) provides for on-demand energy production, (and we have more coal energy under just the State of Illinois, than the entire Middle East has oil energy). Interstate and multinational corporations will not deem these means to be cost-effective alternatives until and unless they are required to pay the true cost of the nation's natural resources that they are using up, burning, and squandering instead.

National Security is Also Enhanced

Without federal interference, local economies could cheaply produce local power using water power, wind power, rebuilt jet engines using inexpensive kerosene, home power production fed back to local grids within the State, thus keeping the grid-destroying acts of aerially blasted bombs or natural events (sunspots) from putting entire regions and economies —even our nation— asunder. The grid, terrorism experts now dread us being the target of aerial nuclear explosions that could put the nation back in the stone age for a decade. But if control and means of production were local, this problem can be contained or eliminated and States sell unused power to other States.

The nation's resources belong to *We the People* and our descendants, not to a handful of corporate giants who have proven to be scoundrels as their stewards.

Technology alone cannot solve our problems. It is time for technological man and natural man to unite and forge a new model of local interests, which will require breaking the strangle-hold of government and its corporate rulers over *We the People*. At present, individuals cannot even create their own energy without difficult-to-obtain government or power monopoly permission. Such is wrong.

These silly laws and rules are not for the benefit of the public, but in service to those whom the lawmakers serve in industry. Having been forgotten by government and corporate entities (or interference) even devastated inner city areas such as Detroit and Cleveland are beginning a transformation to green power and urban food production. Freedom from restraint and a combination of technology with natural life—controlled at local levels—are the answers. The most innovative reformations in these areas are those being brought about by individuals and neighborhoods in spite of the federal governments and corporate interests that throttle them.

Were these corporations unable to bribe our politicians, our nation would immediately transform to one run for the People and by the People, which brings us full circle. Saving our nation, quite literally, begins by taking back control of it from the Progressives and forcing those who represent us to serve us—only.

Our representatives in Washington will immediately begin to look for actual solutions to our nation's problems rather than simply comporting to the whims of the Progressive donors and corporations, to the detriment of the people and destruction of our local economies and environment.

The need for more local decision-making by those who must suffer the environmental damage on the one end of the cycle, and the waste and entropy on the other, has also never been greater—and making the local people the beneficiaries of their natural largesse is the fastest way to make that happen.

Decisions must be made by those closest to their consequences and by those who most suffer the effects of bad ones—and it must be those same people who benefit from wise choices.

That will ultimately be the best political means of keeping power at the State and local level as well. Washington, DC is the last place for decisions affecting local economies and environments to be made except for those that affect Washington.

Congress will become more attuned to their constituents back home and their needs once the link of bondage to the corporations and professional monopolies is severed and bribery is again illegal. They will focus on ways to protect their citizens back home from Progressive ideas and corporate masters, rather than being in their service.

The sustainable way forward is to make all citizens interested parties in the nation's future and protecting its national wealth in resources. Having a stake in their ownership accomplishes that.

Action Plan

Establish natural resource commodities markets based on sustainable model, where all parties are paid for their parts in the process, but the overage, including the sustainability factors and auction profit go into a State or Federal fund—depending on which entity of government controls the land—but belonging to *We the People*, protected from pilferage by the politicians, for use to the benefit of the citizenry and future, rather than to select corporations.

Conclusion

T HE nation simply cannot survive on its current Progressive path. Effectively bankrupt since 1933 and piling up debt at trillions each year, while starting expensive offensive wars and running a costly police state, our nation cannot continue on this course without descending into total tyranny at some point—which should be clear now was the Progressive goal.

Putting people in the untenable position of throwing open the borders, intentionally importing violent gangs and those with ideologies hostile to our own create such chaos and danger—perceived or real does not matter—that people will always beg for the temporary safety of a monarch, dictator, or powerful government. The Progressives know this and are using it.

Unarm the people while doing this, and the task of 'restoring order' is simple. End freedoms and institute the plan you had in mind all along, as there is no one left with the means to resist you. That is why the Founders instituted the Second Amendment and made the military a sum of State units rather than federal. Power was devolved all the way down to the individual and his or her *sword and pistol by the hearth,* ' to quote George Washington, as the ultimate defense of our nation's liberty. There is not a word said about hunting or target shooting. Our weapons and State-operated military units were to protect us from those who would take our liberty, whether from abroad, or from the Swamp, was irrelevant.

History stands as a ready reference as to the outcome one can expect. Governments evolve into being self-enfranchised once checks and balances are removed. Their monopoly on force is used to sustain themselves at any cost, rather than for the benefit of those they were intended to serve. Collapse eventually comes to tyrannies over time, but it can take decades or centuries, which we can ill afford to grant at present. Change must come now while we have a leader with the courage to fight these despicable powers whose goal for 140 years has been to put us back in bondage—to them—the "Elites" as they would call themselves, but the real term for them is 'tyrants'.

The demonic Siamese twins of big government and Progressivism must be separated and chained before they finish destroying the nation.

The first step toward beginning this separation process and decentralization of power is to devolve control back to the States, where it legitimately belongs, closer to *We the People*. No decision that affects how people choose to live amongst themselves is the province of federal government, constitutionally, so long as those local governments do not themselves violate the constitutional rights and privileges of the citizens in the process.

By taking back control of our representatives in Congress from outside entities and corporations as outlined in Chapter 2, and returning the Senate to the control of the States and their legislatures as outlined in Chapter 3; this process can not only be accomplished, it can come about quickly. The return to our beloved Constitution will become a natural process of *devolution* after that.

And that is the beauty of our heritage. We don't need a *revolution*. We had the most beautiful design of government imaginable, and it happens to still be the law. We need a *devolution* to get back to our path and *legal* basis of federal government.

By restoring representation to *We the People* and the States (Chapters 3 and 4, respectively), Chapter 5—getting their hand out of our pockets—becomes possible. Federal government can be forced to reestablish constitutionally prescribed import duties and census-based payments from the States as its sources of revenue. This will have the two-fold effect of restoring jobs to America (and protecting them), while also limiting federal government's income so the beast may once more be restrained, *as designed.*

Chapter 6—Stopping the counterfeit machine and returning to Constitutional Money, will stop artificial booms, busts and bubbles in the economy, where the bankers end up with almost everything in the end. Real money grows organically as real wealth is created. It cannot simply be printed like Federal Reserve notes out of thin air.

Removing the ability of government to rent this illegal, un-backed currency from the Federal Reserve, results in *real* and *sustainable* growth as occurred between the time President Jackson shut down the previous central bank and the Civil War, where this *'species of fraud,'* to use President George Washington's term for central banks, was again used to finance war.

The *grow, grow, grow* consumer culture requires fake money in order to exist. It cannot expand unnaturally without it. By eliminating the junk cash, we eliminate the junk culture. A true, sustainable, real-growth economy can emerge, where quality of life becomes the measure, rather than quantity of junk and trinkets. Real money also has the benefit of being impossible for government to steal through the tax of inflation.

Chapter 7, Putting Pandora back in her box by returning federal government to its Constitutional duties and limits will also occur organically and naturally once Congress is again beholden to its constituents rather than corporate masters and their cash, but this process can be driven forward now by taking action at the State level.

Proposals such as Oklahoma House Joint Resolution 1089 (referenced in Chapter 7), should be presented in all 50 State legislatures. Federal government must be put on notice to cease and desist all activities not listed in Article I, Section 8 of the U.S. Constitution. Government is in breach of its contract with us and must be reminded that its employees are our agents, not our masters, regardless of the lies told by 100+ years of Progressive politicians. James Madison's clear words are impossible to misinterpret for anyone except those with an unconstitutional agenda.

Such notices and actions should be put in process now to drive the movement in Washington. Politicians will only get on board with change if they see that the game is over, and *We the People* have had enough—either by direct legislative notice or Convention of States.

Chapter 8, regarding returning the 'Most powerful man in the world' to the one authorized in our Constitution, will be difficult until Congress has been retaken by *We the People*. The presidents have been allowed their illegal Executive Orders, unauthorized Justice Department, their 16 unconstitutional spy agencies, their FBIs, NSAs and gangs of Progressives to run them, because Congress has itself been so far out of constitutional bounds that the pot could hardly call the kettle black.

As then Chairman of the House Judiciary Committee, James Clyburn said in 2008 , *"Almost nothing Congress does today can find root in the Constitution."* It's high time for this to change—and it can only happen while the Progressives are back on their heels and Donald Trump is at the helm.

Chapter 9, 'What do we do with Andy' regarding the return of our federal Judicial Branch to its Constitutional scope and function won't happen until we've had several funerals of Supreme Court Justices—and a complete change of heart in Congress—but that can happen. All but three of the nine are collecting Social Security or already seem to have one foot in whatever place Progressives believe they go after death, so opportunities can present themselves.

Meanwhile, Congress must follow the example of every other nation on earth that claims to be free, and establish elected Ombudsmen courts in every federal district with the power to prosecute bad actors of government as well as to undo their injustices to *We the People.* Waiting on federal courts or 'Andy' to undo the injustice they now commit in almost 8 out of 10 cases, has proven useless, and Congress ended our rights to challenge that lawlessness, for all intents and purposes, when they illegally suspended our constitutional right to *habeas corpus* in 1996.

Term limits for Congressmen, Senators, federal judges, and Supreme Court Justices should soon follow—and that needs to be added to the Convention of States agenda. If it wasn't unconstitutional to limit the presidents' term in office in Amendment 22, it certainly isn't to stop others from living off of us—or abusing us— for life.

Putting an unaccountable, unelected person on federal court benches (for life) has proven to be a very, very bad idea. The current Roberts court and its members are also there for life, and none of them appear to have ever read the Constitution as James Madison wrote it, so again, President Trump has the chance to absolutely shake it up by putting some real constitutionalists and historians on the bench to offset the powdered wig class. At the rate Trump is going, he might outlive them all—and six more years is a long time.

The best long-term solution for our nation is to find ways to replace them. We need some sensible, non-lawyer, constitutional scholars as Supreme Court Justices, not this endless string of attorneys who prefer to depend on bad *stare decisis* (precedent) and their own pettifogging instead of James Madison's clear words in our contract—the U.S. Constitution —and some of them deserve to be removed for what they have done to it.

A non-lawyer wrote the Constitution, I will say again, so it certainly does not require a lawyer to interpret its plain and clear language. The

Supreme Court needs to also get back ahead of the game, even if they have to move back into the basement of the Capitol to do it.

Bad legislation needs to be stopped before it becomes bad law and Congress should be required to state the precise clause of the Constitution that allows them to do what they are doing, and how that duty is better handled at the federal level, so these unconstitutional acts stop being slipped through, but the Supreme Court must quit its own malfeasance by making law instead of following it. Like failing to enforce the Constitution by finding words not in it (such as 'corporation' for example) and granting powers never envisioned in that document (like giving them rights of 'citizenship' for another example) are actual, constitutional cause for removal under the 'good behavior' clause in Article III.

If you are in charge of a contract and working to protect the party that made it (We the People) and take it upon yourself as its guardian to disregard parts you don't like, add clauses and powers not in it—without ever asking for permission from the party for whom you work? Well, that is not 'good behavior.' That is criminal conduct under anyone's understanding of legal or fiduciary responsibilities. Send the suckers to the rest home early and put in some people who have read the Constitution and will follow it. It is that simple.

And with a Judicial budget of $7.0 billion for 2017—the budget of nations rather than a department— they could spare a few people to review bills out of committee and opine on their constitutionality upfront before they come to a final vote, rather than wasting more resources years later to overturn them. If Congress passes them anyway, the Court can be prepared to rule them null and void before they do harm.

Chapter 10 regarding restoring the military to Constitutional boundaries (Time to Bring Johnny Home), is not a recommendation to eliminate readiness or strength, as detractors will inevitably claim, but to make our military better—and legal. We were never meant to be a Progressive Empire with legions used to conquer nations, people (and their resources) abroad, only a republic with a defensive force like the most prosperous, peaceful, cleanest, *and* safest nation on earth, which was used by our Founders as our example. This model has worked for Switzerland for half a millennia in the middle of the bloodiest continent of that time period, and it can certainly work for us, isolated and protected by two vast oceans, with the world's strongest navy.

The military of today, through no fault of the fine men and women who serve in it, does not serve its intended purpose. It is little more than an armed escort for transnational corporations and Progressive causes to impose their order on others. It is too costly, has made us a pariah nation with most of the world, and is unconstitutional. We would be far better defended, and have far less reason for defense, if the federal armies reverted to State-controlled militias (Swiss model) as prescribed by our Founders, to be called upon in time of declared war.

Chapter 11, Putting the Corporate Genie Back in the Bottle, is the underlying context of the whole plan. Our representatives were stolen from us almost 140 years ago by the predecessors of today's robber barons. Our currency has been debauched and our nation swallowed whole by these evil forces calling themselves "Progressive" but whose own history and words prove their goal is domination. We've gone from a peaceful republic to a warring empire in their service. Our nation is bankrupt and in decline with government's heel on our necks in the name of security, as disclosed by NSA contractor Edward Snowden, and more recently seen in the conspiracy by every single leader of every single snoop and arrest agency in federal government joining a Progressive conspiracy to take out our president. It's time for them and their unconstitutional agencies to be shuttered.

In answer to "What do we do about Andy?", we try him and the rest for treason after their trials for denying civil rights to thousands of citizens and a President of the United States under control of law (18 U.S.C.

§§241,242) which by my estimation would be at least three lifetimes in prison for each of them, followed by execution.

I choose not to be their serf any longer. I will not have my children and grandchildren enslaved by them or sent to fight for their Progressive power plays and die in foreign lands. Let them send their own children, or do it themselves. I want to live in a free and peaceful nation, as is my inalienable right to do, which means one of us is going to have to go. I've already had to leave but it is time to take a stand. I want my country back.

Chapter 12, and our Sustainable Way Forward will come naturally to a free people no longer controlled by forces outside of their own communities and regions. Each State must decide for itself how to live, as intended: fifty separate experiments in self-government. Several States are re-asserting their sovereignty by refusing to enforce federal government's bizarre marijuana laws.

Regardless of one's opinion on marijuana, for example, it's a positive step in the right direction, in my opinion. I am against its use, personally, but will fight for another's right to do so, if they so choose. And this is a great example of how Progressivism and corporate control has worked in our nation, which is why I bring it up.

In the nation's early days, growing hemp was required by the federal government of any landowner whose property was over a certain size to make rope for the navy. Now it's the cause of 49.8% of arrests and federal government wastes $42 billion each year trying to stop its citizens from using and growing it. It's a natural weed, and the number one cash crop of 12 States. Ridiculous federal abuses like this will ultimately lead to change.

And it was outlawed, not because of its non-pharma powers to heal or the recreational pleasures it provided as a substitute for alcohol, but because of major political donations from international corporations who wanted the contract to make and sell artificial fibre products, such as rope, to our navy. Hemp had to be banned to make that possible—even though it was probably a better and definitely more renewable product —so the corporations used their purse power to have it outlawed and the Progressives then disenfranchised almost 35 million American of their right to vote or participate in the American dream, by convicting them of its possession or use—in service to their corporate partners, not us.

Ultimately, it is a good bet—assuming we can take our country back from these people—that we can keep this all from happening again by incorporating every American into the ownership of their State's resources. That will act to make everyone a steward of the land. The great wealth of this nation can and should be shared by all those in it, giving everyone a stake. By applying free market and economic principles to the sustainable model described, this great land will have the means of supporting many more generations of Americans.

While it may seem almost impossible at present that these dramatic changes could come about swiftly in the United States, I respectfully disagree—now that we have someone at the helm with the courage to do it. Just one man (with large, previously used, cohones) can change the world, just as Ronald Reagan did in the 1980s.

Those who were alive and watched the Soviet Union crumble under far less debt than we now have in August of 1991 know first-hand that it can happen and fast. The speed with which that world power collapsed was a shock to everyone, but this is the natural, historic end to overly-powerful, top-heavy, militaristic, federal governments. The fact that we are us rather than them makes no difference to history or the immutable laws of economics, if we do not change.

Perhaps a better lesson to America's weak, feckless and Progressive leaders of the past century than the Soviet Union's collapse is how swiftly their grasp on the nation can slip away from them.

One brave man in The White House—Ronald Reagan—and the leadership of our greatest foe—Michaił Gorbaczow— seeing that he would not back down, caused the end of Communism. It brought down the Berlin Wall, its symbol, and The Soviet Union, its power broker. The ultimate hero of Progressives was the Soviet Union, and President Reagan brought about the Progressives' first major defeat on the world stage since their inception.

Now its time for President Trump to take out that same group who planned, funded, and propped up the Soviet Union—the Progressives.

The winds of change are upon the world and Americans are not that far from finding power within themselves to take back their rights, their courts, and their government, from the same usurpers in Washington who have overthrown and supported tyrants in other lands under the rule of American Progressives.

What is unique about this nation and what may yet save it, is the fact that we have a working plan for government, which is perhaps the finest and purest ever devised. It is also still the law. Our leaders just stopped following it.

Our current financial insolvency, corrupt system of justice, unfair courts, packed prisons, pointless wars, as well as loss of industry and jobs are all curable now, if government simply returns to its lawful contract with *We the People,* as President Trump is trying to force them to do. That is all that is required.

We don't have to create a new government. We don't have to set up commissions to study the problems. We don't have to waste a moment, which is good, because we do not have a moment to waste.

Our design of government was basically perfect. We don't have to reinvent it, we just have to go back to it. All that is required to bring us back from the brink of disaster is to return to that design, get back on the path, and force the federal government to live by our contract.

We the People made a deal with government, and that "deal" was the United States Constitution. Our leaders are in severe breach of it, not us.

Want our nation to stop hemorrhaging money? Restrict federal government to its duties listed in the contract (Article I, Section 8). End of problem.

Want peace? Return to a constitutional military, which would require unelected spooks to quit murdering elected foreign officials and pillaging other nations. Force them to leave everyone the hell alone, and you've got peace overnight, unless someone messes with us first. Then we blow them off the map to let everyone know what happens. End of problem.

Want jobs? Shut down the Progressive red-tape machine and put back our main source of constitutional revenue, import duties, which were designed to protect our domestic industries and jobs—just like President Trump is doing—and America will become a boom nation in terms of manufacturing and employment in a period of months. Remember, no nation has ever free-traded its way to prosperity in history, and only the free-traders themselves are the beneficiaries of such madness. Put back this constitutional source of revenue and our nation will quickly return to full employment.

Want to end money in politics and return to a truly representative republic? It's simple. Just do it. It is so easy. If only living, breathing citizens residing within the candidates' jurisdiction or district could donate money or services to those politicians, as was once the law, we are there immediately. No corporate money to buy them, no PACs to lure them; no unions to threaten them, not even the two political parties could control the national agenda. If only individuals registered to vote or living permanently in the candidate's district can contribute to them, we're back to having representatives who actually represent us, in one day. End of problem.

Want to keep our country from being stolen from us again? It can be done in three easy steps and it does not require a revolution. First, end federal government's self-granted power to tax individuals, by repealing the Sixteenth Amendment (or having it voided, due to the irregularities admitted in its implementation in 1913). Second, turn off the Federal Reserve's fake money machine by repealing legal tender laws and the Glass-Owen (Federal Reserve) Act. Go back to real money and allow people to create their own means of exchange. Third, return to the constitutionally required method of choosing Senators, who will guard the powers of the people and States from federal government's future attempts to usurp them.

If the United States federal government is required to live within the confines of constitutional sources of revenue (import duties, imposts, and excise taxes, with any shortfall allocated to the States based on the census) and we're using real money, government can only cause so much trouble. With the Senators once again elected by the State legislatures, things will stay in order this time.

Corporations do have their place, but corporations are *not* constitutionally protected from taxation as individuals are under Article I, Section 9. Once the anomaly of their citizenship is removed either legislatively or judicially, a straight 30% federal tax should remain on those operating across state lines or international borders, and whatever the States in which they were incorporated or operate set as their corporate rate. Those who wish to enjoy the benefits of corporate status and its protections can pay for it.

By having this tax on corporations, small entrepreneurs, privately owned businesses, and proprietorships, can once again flourish and compete, just as domestic industries will once more be competitive with foreign producers when import duties are re-imposed on foreign-produced products. The playing field is then leveled and *We the People* are the beneficiaries this time, rather than *Them the Corporations* or the Soros-backed ilk who have tried for a century to take us over—and almost did.

And so the big companies don't think this is too prohibitive, this 30% corporate tax might even be considered the big corporation's *public service* requirement that justifies their existence.

As can easily be seen, the United States does not necessarily need a *revolution* outside of the one we had on November 8th of 2016. From here on out, we just need a leader of our *devolution*. Devolution is not regressive in this case; it is simply going back to what worked.

The beauty of this in the case of the United States is that we would be returning to our roots and living by our own laws for a change. This would act to put the true owners of the nation, *We the People*, back in charge of our lives and return us to being its natural beneficiaries. That would be quite a revolution, and nothing could be more American.

Perhaps our greatest challenge is also the easiest, which is taking back our courts from the prosecutors, lawyers, and judges who now control them through craft and deceit. Juries comprised of *We the People* are the rightful custodians of the courts and we must reassert our control over them. We not only have the power to judge the facts in the cases brought before us, we have the power to rule against any unfair, unreasonable, or unconstitutional law being applied in them, by refusing to convict those charged under such law.

Just one juror is all it takes to nullify those bad laws and there is nothing any judge or prosecutor can do about it. We have the authority to completely ignore any instruction from any judge on any point of law and do what is right instead.[3]

---

[3] *By voting "not guilty", the law is nullified in a case, and that decision by a juror or jury is unreviewable. Even if someone is guilty of a bad law, it is the juror's and jury's duty to rule against that law by refusing to convict the person charged under it. This is part of our system of checks and balances.*

In a jury box, you are the law and as a juror, you have more power than the President, Congress, any legislature, or the United States Supreme Court.

All we as a people have to do is reassert that truly awesome power and our courts will change overnight.

People charged under bad law should not suffer it, and those convicted of any crime not allowed to be punished by federal courts, must have their rights as citizens restored immediately, including the right to vote.

That is an idea for our new president. Re-enfranchise those who have lost their citizenship rights to the Progressive's incarceration machine and you will have their hearts and souls for the remainder of their days. I remember as a child every black member of our small, North Carolina town, being a follower of "The Party of Lincoln," which was the Republican Party, but overnight in early July of 1964, every one of them became a diehard Democrat for life.

Why? Because with The Civil Rights Act of 1964, the Democrats gave back the respect and citizenship rights they had taken away from black citizens during their Progressive control of the federal government and restored them.

A person whose rights of citizenship and equal treatment under law is restored to them, will clearly follow the leader who had the courage or foresight to be the person to make it happen.

The Progressives have disenfranchised over 71 million Americans of their right to vote and defend themselves just since I was in college. Imagine if the President gave them back their dignity and power as citizens. What would you do? From my own observations and history, I'll tell you what you would do. You would follow that man and his lead for the rest of your life and encourage your children and grandchildren to do so as well, just like Black Americans followed Lincoln for 100 years, and switched overnight to the Democratic Party that had taken those rights and freedoms from them a century before.

That's one in every four adult Americans, Sir, who could be voting for the man who liberated them according to the Department of Justices' own numbers.[4] Just since rappers Kanye West and P. Diddy came out in favor of President Trump's positive impact on the black community, his support among Black Americans has doubled from 11% to 22%—in two weeks. Free the illegally incarcerated and unlawfully disenfranchised, and you will change the political world overnight.

You would crush the Progressives with such a landslide, and harness the largest disenfranchised group of people in our nation's history to your cause. 71 million is a big number, Sir.

Combined, these simple changes can restore our country to being a peaceful, prosperous, egalitarian, and free society. That is what we were meant to be rather than the biggest, meanest bully on the planet where only a handful of Elites and an army of unelected bureaucrats under their control rule and own the land. That is what we rebelled from once before, and it is clearly time to finish the revolution we started in 2016.

Not a single shot has to be fired or a single drop of blood shed this time. We just have to make the current batch of tyrants understand that their game is over, and they are going to have to live by our contract once again. Government is going to have to follow the law-the ultimate law-our Constitution, or Washington Square may soon look like Tahrir Square did in February of 2011. It *can* happen here if they don't wake up soon. It *must* happen here, if they resist our calls for lawful government. Better yet, have a limited Convention of States, whose purpose and purview can only be to limit rather than expand federal government and bring them back into line.

---

[4] *BNA Criminal Law Reporter,* by Eric M. Fish. May 19th edition, 2010 (Vol. 87, No. 7)

Our ancestors wrote to the last tyrant from whom we separated on July 4, 1776, "*That whenever any Form of Government becomes destructive of these ends [Life, Liberty and the pursuit of Happiness], it is the Right of the People to alter or to abolish it, and to institute new Government, laying its foundation on such principles and organizing its powers in such form, as to them shall seem most likely to affect their Safety and Happiness.*"

Those words were written by Thomas Jefferson, and can be found in our Declaration of Independence. The ills and injustices put upon our forefathers by King George III, pale in comparison to the abuses heaped on the American public by 100 years of Progressivism, and it is clearly time to let them know that we have reached a satiety. It is time to go back to who we are supposed to be. It is time for America to return to being the shining light of liberty on the hill for others to follow, rather than the world's largest penal colony, with more laws, police agencies, prisons, and prisoners, than any (other) tyrant in mankind's history.

It is time for us to once again live quietly in peace as we were intended to do, rather than murdering, invading, and intimidating those living in other nations, while being spied upon in our own homes by our Progressives in government. Those are not powers under federal purview or authority and those who exercise them in our name need to go.

It is time for us to get back to our own form of government, which is a *republic*, where we elect representatives, but there are certain inalienable rights that no majority can vote away, and no government can take from us. It is time for the American Devolution. It is time for us to return to our beloved Constitution.

It is late in the day, but it can still be done peacefully. Let us pull together and save our country now, while that peaceful way is still open to us— and we have a leader dedicated to taking us there.

VIVA LA DEVOLUTION!
Howell Woltz
May 29, 2018

About the Author

Howell W. Woltz, journalist and author, graduated from the University of Virginia in 1975 with a degree in economics, attended MBA School at Wake Forest University, and studied at Caledonia University in Glasgow, Scotland. He left the United States in 2015 after threats from U.S. officials seeking to silence him for speaking out about Progressive policies and judicial corruption in America. He now lives with his wife, Dr. Magdalena Woltz in Warsaw, Poland.

Mr. Woltz began speaking out against the the Progressive movement and its inherent dangers in 1977 [see article on next page]. He has advised presidents at home and prime ministers abroad, but his passion throughout has been The United States Constitution and how his home nation can return to it.

His most recent bestseller, *Justice Restored: 10 steps to end mass incarceration in America*, (2016) is currently being used by American judicial reform advocates at the national level.

Restoring America: by Returning to our Constitution, is the culmination of 40 years of study on what went wrong in America, and how it can be set right again by returning federal government to the strict limits of its contract with *We the People*. That contract is The Constitution of the United States—and while Donald Trump, the new leader in America—is the first willing to do so in decades, Mr. Woltz advocates for a return to its requirements.

Howell W. Woltz, The International Centre for Justice. Bukowińska 2, m. 194, 02-703, Warsaw, Poland. Tel. +48 604 900 183, howell@justicerestored.com

Howell Woltz (in tie) is surrounded by students seeking information after giving his talk on waning freedoms at Mount Airy High School [TIMES Photo–Maloy]

Woltz Fears Loss Of Freedoms

Appendix A
The United States Constitution

We the People of the United States, in Order to form a more perfect Union, establish Justice, insure domestic Tranquility, provide for the common defence, promote the general Welfare, and secure the Blessings of Liberty to ourselves and our Posterity, do ordain and establish this Constitution for the United States of America.

Article I

Section 1. All legislative Powers herein granted shall be vested in a Congress of the United States, which shall consist of a Senate and House of Representatives.

Section 2. The House of Representatives shall be composed of Members chosen every second Year by the People of the several States, and the Electors in each State shall have the Qualifications requisite for Electors of the most numerous Branch of the State Legislature.

No Person shall be a Representative who shall not have attained to the age of twenty five Years, and been seven Years a Citizen of the United States, and who shall not, when elected, be an Inhabitant of that State in which he shall be chosen.

Representatives and direct Taxes shall be apportioned among the several States which may be included within this Union, according to their respective Numbers, which shall be determined by adding to the whole Number of free Persons, including those bound to Service for a Term of Years, and excluding Indians not taxed, three fifths of all other Persons. The actual Enumeration shall be made within three Years after the first Meeting of the Congress of the United States, and within every subsequent Term of ten Years, in such Manner as they shall by Law direct. The Number of Representatives shall not exceed one for every thirty Thousand, but each State shall have at Least one Representative; and until such enumeration shall be made, the State of New Hampshire shall be entitled to chuse three, Massachusetts eight, Rhode-Island and Providence Plantations one, Connecticut five, New-York six, New Jersey four, Pennsylvania eight, Delaware one, Maryland six, Virginia ten, North Carolina five, South Carolina five, and Georgia three.

When vacancies happen in the Representation from any State, the Executive Authority thereof shall issue Writs of Election to fill such Vacancies.

The House of Representatives shall chuse their Speaker and other Officers; and shall have the sole Power of Impeachment.

Section 3. The Senate of the United States shall be composed of two Senators from each State, chosen by the Legislature thereof, for six Years; and each Senator shall have one Vote.

Immediately after they shall be assembled in Consequence of the first Election, they shall be divided as equally as may be into three Classes. The Seats of the Senators of the first Class shall be vacated at the Expiration of the second Year, of the second Class at the Expiration of the fourth Year, and the third Class at the Expiration of the sixth Year, so that one third may be chosen every second Year; and if Vacancies happen by Resignation, or otherwise, during the Recess of the Legislature of any State, the Executive thereof may make temporary Appointments until the next Meeting of the Legislature, which shall then fill such Vacancies.

No Person shall be a Senator who shall not have attained to the Age of thirty Years, and been nine Years a Citizen of the United States and who shall not, when elected, be an Inhabitant of that State for which he shall be chosen.

The Vice President of the United States shall be President of the Senate, but shall have no Vote, unless they be equally divided.

The Senate shall chuse their other Officers, and also a President pro-tempore, in the Absence of the Vice President, or when he shall exercise the Office of President of the United States.

The Senate shall have the sole Power to try all Impeachments. When sitting for that Purpose, they shall be on Oath or Affirmation. When the President of the United States is tried, the Chief Justice shall preside: And no Person shall be convicted without the Concurrence of two thirds of the Members present.

Judgment in Cases of Impeachment shall not extend further than to removal from Office, and disqualification to hold and enjoy any Office of Honor, Trust or Profit under the United States: but the Party convicted shall nevertheless be liable and subject to Indictment, Trial, Judgment and Punishment, according to Law.

Section 4. The Times, Places and Manner of holding Elections for Senators and Representatives, shall be prescribed in each State by the Legislature thereof; but the Congress may at any time by Law make or alter such Regulations, except as to the Places of chusing Senators.

The Congress shall assemble at least once in every Year, and such Meeting shall be on the first Monday in December, unless they shall by Law appoint a different Day.

Section 5. Each House shall be the Judge of the Elections, Returns and Qualifications of its own Members, and a Majority of each shall constitute a Quorum to do Business; but a smaller Number may adjourn from day to day, and may be authorized to compel the Attendance of absent Members, in such Manner, and under such Penalties as each House may provide.

Each House may determine the Rules of its Proceedings, punish its Members for disorderly Behaviour, and, with the Concurrence of two thirds, expel a Member.

Each House shall keep a Journal of its Proceedings, and from time to time publish the same, excepting such Parts as may in their Judgment require Secrecy; and the Yeas and Nays of the Members of either House on any question shall, at the Desire of one fifth of those Present, be entered on the Journal.

Neither House, during the Session of Congress, shall, without the Consent of the other, adjourn for more than three days, nor to any other Place than that in which the two Houses shall be sitting.

Section 6. The Senators and Representatives shall receive a Compensation for their Services, to be ascertained by Law, and paid out of the Treasury of the United States. They shall in all Cases, except Treason, Felony and Breach of the Peace, be privileged from Arrest during their Attendance at the Session of their respective Houses, and in going to and returning from the same; and for any Speech or Debate in either House, they shall not be questioned in any other Place.

No Senator or Representative shall, during the Time for which he was elected, be appointed to any civil Office under the Authority of the United States, which shall have been created, or the Emoluments whereof shall have been encreased during such time: and no Person holding any Office under the United States, shall be a Member of either House during his Continuance in Office.

Section 7. All Bills for raising Revenue shall originate in the House of Representatives; but the Senate may propose or concur with Amendments as on other Bills. Every Bill which shall have passed the House of Representatives and the Senate, shall, before it become a Law, be presented to the President of the United States; if he approve he shall sign it, but if not he shall return it, with his Objections to that House in which it shall have originated, who shall enter the Objections at large on their Journal, and proceed to reconsider it. If after such Reconsideration two thirds of that House shall agree to pass the Bill, it shall be sent, together with the Objections, to the other House, by which it shall likewise be reconsidered, and if approved by two thirds of that House, it shall become a Law. But in all such Cases the Votes of both Houses shall be determined by Yeas and Nays, and the Names of the Persons voting for and against the Bill shall be entered on the Journal of each House respectively. If any Bill shall not be returned by the President within ten Days (Sundays excepted) after it shall have been presented to him, the Same shall be a Law, in like Manner as if he had signed it, unless the Congress by their Adjournment prevent its Return, in which Case it shall not be a Law.

Every Order, Resolution, or Vote to which the Concurrence of the Senate and House of Representatives may be necessary (except on a question of Adjournment) shall be presented to the President of the United States; and before the Same shall take Effect, shall be approved by him, or being disapproved by him, shall be repassed by two thirds of the Senate and House of Representatives, according to the Rules and Limitations prescribed in the Case of a Bill.

Section 8. The Congress shall have Power To lay and collect Taxes, Duties, Imposts and Excises, to pay the Debts and provide for the common Defence and general Welfare of the United States; but all Duties, Imposts and Excises shall be uniform throughout the United States; To borrow Money on the credit of the United States;

To regulate Commerce with foreign Nations, and among the several States, and with the Indian Tribes;

To establish an uniform Rule of Naturalization, and uniform Laws on the subject of Bankruptcies throughout the United States;

To coin Money, regulate the Value thereof, and of foreign Coin, and fix the Standard of Weights and Measures;

To provide for the Punishment of counterfeiting the Securities and current Coin of the United States;

To establish Post Offices and post Roads;

To promote the Progress of Science and useful Arts, by securing for limited Times to Authors and Inventors the exclusive Right to their respective Writings and Discoveries;

To constitute Tribunals inferior to the Supreme Court;

To define and punish Piracies and Felonies committed on the high Seas, and Offences against the Law of Nations;

To declare War, grant Letters of Marque and Reprisal, and make Rules concerning Captures on Land and Water;

To raise and support Armies, but no Appropriation of Money to that Use shall be for a longer Term than two Years;

To provide and maintain a Navy;

To make Rules for the Government and Regulation of the land and naval Forces;

To provide for calling forth the Militia to execute the Laws of the Union, suppress Insurrections and repel Invasions;

To provide for organizing, arming, and disciplining, the Militia, and for governing such Part of them as may be employed in the Service of the

United States, reserving to the States respectively, the Appointment of the Officers, and the Authority of training the Militia according to the discipline prescribed by Congress;

To exercise exclusive Legislation in all Cases whatsoever, over such District (not exceeding ten Miles square) as may, by Cession of particular States, and the Acceptance of Congress, become the Seat of the Government of the United States, and to exercise like Authority over all Places purchased by the Consent of the Legislature of the State in which the Same shall be, for the Erection of Forts, Magazines, Arsenals, dock-Yards, and other needful Buildings;–And

To make all Laws which shall be necessary and proper for carrying into Execution the foregoing Powers, and all other Powers vested by this Constitution in the Government of the United States, or in any Department or Officer thereof.

Section 9. The Migration or Importation of such Persons as any of the States now existing shall think proper to admit, shall not be prohibited by the Congress prior to the Year one thousand eight hundred and eight, but a Tax or duty may be imposed on such Importation, not exceeding ten dollars for each Person.

The Privilege of the Writ of Habeas Corpus shall not be suspended, unless when in Cases of Rebellion or Invasion the public Safety may require it.

No Bill of Attainder or ex post facto Law shall be passed.

No Capitation, or other direct, Tax shall be laid, unless in Proportion to the Census or Enumeration herein before directed to be taken.

No Tax or Duty shall be laid on Articles exported from any State.

No Preference shall be given by any Regulation of Commerce or Revenue to the Ports of one State over those of another: nor shall Vessels bound to, or from, one State, be obliged to enter, clear or pay Duties in another.

No Money shall be drawn from the Treasury, but in Consequence of Appropriations made by Law; and a regular Statement and Account of Receipts and Expenditures of all public Money shall be published from time to time.

No Title of Nobility shall be granted by the United States: And no Person holding any Office of Profit or Trust under them, shall, without the Consent of the Congress, accept of any present, Emolument, Office, or Title, of any kind whatever, from any King, Prince, or foreign State.

Section 10. No State shall enter into any Treaty, Alliance, or Confederation; grant Letters of Marque and Reprisal; coin Money; emit Bills of Credit; make any Thing but gold and silver Coin a Tender in Payment of Debts; pass any Bill of Attainder, ex post facto Law, or Law impairing the Obligation of Contracts, or grant any Title of Nobility.

No State shall, without the Consent of the Congress, lay any Imposts or Duties on Imports or Exports, except what may be absolutely necessary for executing it's inspection Laws: and the net Produce of all Duties and Imposts, laid by any State on Imports or Exports, shall be for the Use of the Treasury of the United States; and all such Laws shall be subject to the Revision and Control of the Congress.

No State shall, without the Consent of Congress, lay any Duty of Tonnage, keep Troops, or Ships of War in time of Peace, enter into any Agreement or Compact with another State, or with a foreign Power, or engage in War, unless actually invaded, or in such imminent Danger as will not admit of delay.

Article II

Section 1. The executive Power shall be vested in a President of the United States of America. He shall hold his Office during the Term of four Years, and together with the Vice President, chosen for the same Term, be elected, as follows:

Each State shall appoint, in such Manner as the Legislature thereof may direct, a Number of Electors, equal to the whole Number of Senators and Representatives to which the State may be entitled in the Congress: but no Senator or Representative, or Person holding an Office of Trust or Profit under the United States, shall be appointed an Elector.

The Electors shall meet in their respective States, and vote by Ballot for two Persons, of whom one at least shall not be an Inhabitant of the same State with themselves. And they shall make a List of all the Persons voted for, and of the Number of Votes for each; which List they shall sign and certify, and transmit sealed to the Seat of the Government of the United States, directed to the President of the Senate. The President of the Senate shall, in the Presence of the Senate and House of Representatives, open all the Certificates, and the Votes shall then be counted. The Person having the greatest Number of Votes shall be the President, if such Number be a Majority of the whole Number of Electors appointed; and if there be more than one who have such Majority, and have an equal Number of Votes, then the House of Representatives shall immediately chuse by Ballot one of them for President; and if no Person have a Majority, then from the five highest on the List the said House shall in like Manner chuse the President. But in chusing the President, the Votes shall be taken by States, the Representation from each State having one Vote; A quorum for this Purpose shall consist of a Member or Members from two thirds of the States, and a Majority of all the States shall be necessary to a Choice. In every Case, after the Choice of the President, the Person having the greatest Number of Votes of the Electors shall be the Vice President. But if there should remain two or more who have equal Votes, the Senate shall chuse from them by Ballot the Vice President.

The Congress may determine the Time of chusing the Electors, and the Day on which they shall give their Votes; which Day shall be the same throughout the United States.

No Person except a natural born Citizen, or a Citizen of the United States, at the time of the Adoption of this Constitution, shall be eligible to the Office of President; neither shall any Person be eligible to that Office who shall not have attained to the Age of thirty five Years, and been fourteen Years a Resident within the United States.

In Case of the Removal of the President from Office, or of his Death, Resignation, or Inability to discharge the Powers and Duties of the said Office, the Same shall devolve on the Vice President, and the Congress may by Law provide for the Case of Removal, Death, Resignation or Inability, both of the President and Vice President, declaring what Officer shall then act as President, and such Officer shall act accordingly, until the Disability be removed, or a President shall be elected.

The President shall, at stated Times, receive for his Services, a Compensation, which shall neither be increased nor diminished during the Period for which he shall have been elected, and he shall not receive within that Period any other Emolument from the United States, or any of them.

Before he enter on the Execution of his Office, he shall take the following Oath or Affirmation:—"I do solemnly swear (or affirm) that I will faithfully execute the Office of President of the United States, and will to the best of my Ability, preserve, protect and defend the Constitution of the United States."

Section 2. The President shall be Commander in Chief of the Army and Navy of the United States, and of the Militia of the several States, when called into the actual Service of the United States; he may require the Opinion, in writing, of the principal Officer in each of the executive Departments, upon any Subject relating to the Duties of their respective

Offices, and he shall have Power to grant Reprieves and Pardons for Offences against the United States, except in Cases of Impeachment.

He shall have Power, by and with the Advice and Consent of the Senate, to make Treaties, provided two thirds of the Senators present concur; and he shall nominate, and by and with the Advice and Consent of the Senate, shall appoint Ambassadors, other public Ministers and Consuls, Judges of the supreme Court, and all other Officers of the United States, whose Appointments are not herein otherwise provided for, and which shall be established by Law: but the Congress may by Law vest the Appointment of such inferior Officers, as they think proper, in the President alone, in the Courts of Law, or in the Heads of Departments.

The President shall have Power to fill up all Vacancies that may happen during the Recess of the Senate, by granting Commissions which shall expire at the End of their next Session.

Section 3. He shall from time to time give to the Congress Information of the State of the Union, and recommend to their Consideration such Measures as he shall judge necessary and expedient; he may, on extraordinary Occasions, convene both Houses, or either of them, and in Case of Disagreement between them, with Respect to the Time of Adjournment, he may adjourn them to such Time as he shall think proper; he shall receive Ambassadors and other public Ministers; he shall take Care that the Laws be faithfully executed, and shall Commission all the Officers of the United States.

Section 4. The President, Vice President and all civil Officers of the United States, shall be removed from Office on Impeachment for, and Conviction of, Treason, Bribery, or other high Crimes and Misdemeanors.

Article III

Section 1. The judicial Power of the United States, shall be vested in one supreme Court, and in such inferior Courts as the Congress may from time to time ordain and establish. The Judges, both of the supreme and inferior Courts, shall hold their Offices during good Behaviour, and shall, at stated Times, receive for their Services, a Compensation, which shall not be diminished during their Continuance in Office.

Section 2. The judicial Power shall extend to all Cases, in Law and Equity, arising under this Constitution, the Laws of the United States, and Treaties made, or which shall be made, under their Authority;–to all Cases affecting Ambassadors, other public Ministers and Consuls;–to all Cases of admiralty and maritime Jurisdiction;–to Controversies to which the United States shall be a Party;–to Controversies between two or more States;–between a State and Citizens of another State;–between Citizens of different States;–between Citizens of the same State claiming Lands under Grants of different States, and between a State, or the Citizens thereof, and foreign States, Citizens or Subjects.

In all Cases affecting Ambassadors, other public Ministers and Consuls, and those in which a State shall be Party, the Supreme Court shall have original Jurisdiction. In all the other Cases before mentioned, the Supreme Court shall have appellate Jurisdiction, both as to Law and Fact, with such Exceptions, and under such Regulations as the Congress shall make.

The Trial of all Crimes, except in Cases of Impeachment, shall be by Jury; and such Trial shall be held in the State where the said Crimes shall have been committed; but when not committed within any State, the Trial shall be at such Place or Places as the Congress may by Law have directed.

Section 3. Treason against the United States, shall consist only in levying War against them, or in adhering to their Enemies, giving them Aid and Comfort. No Person shall be convicted of Treason unless on the Testimony of two Witnesses to the same overt Act, or on Confession in open Court.

The Congress shall have Power to declare the Punishment of Treason, but no Attainder of Treason shall work Corruption of Blood, or Forfeiture except during the Life of the Person attainted.

Article IV

Section 1. Full Faith and Credit shall be given in each State to the public Acts, Records, and judicial Proceedings of every other State. And the Congress may by general Laws prescribe the Manner in which such Acts, Records, and Proceedings shall be proved, and the Effect thereof.

Section 2. The Citizens of each State shall be entitled to all Privileges and Immunities of Citizens in the several States.

A Person charged in any State with Treason, Felony, or other Crime, who shall flee from Justice, and be found in another State, shall on Demand of the executive Authority of the State from which he fled, be delivered up, to be removed to the State having Jurisdiction of the Crime.

No Person held to Service or Labour in one State, under the Laws thereof, escaping into another, shall, in Consequence of any Law or Regulation therein, be discharged from such Service or Labour, but shall be delivered up on Claim of the Party to whom such Service or Labour may be due.

Section 3. New States may be admitted by the Congress into this Union; but no new States shall be formed or erected within the Jurisdiction of any other State; nor any State be formed by the Junction of two or more States, or Parts of States, without the Consent of the Legislatures of the States concerned as well as of the Congress.

The Congress shall have Power to dispose of and make all needful Rules and Regulations respecting the Territory or other Property belonging to the United States; and nothing in this Constitution shall be so construed as to Prejudice any Claims of the United States, or of any particular State.

Section 4. The United States shall guarantee to every State in this Union a Republican Form of Government, and shall protect each of them against Invasion; and on Application of the Legislature, or of the Executive (when the Legislature cannot be convened) against domestic Violence.

Article V

The Congress, whenever two thirds of both Houses shall deem it necessary, shall propose Amendments to this Constitution, or, on the Application of the Legislatures of two thirds of the several States, shall call a Convention for proposing Amendments, which, in either Case, shall be valid to all Intents and Purposes, as Part of this Constitution, when ratified by the Legislatures of three fourths of the several States, or by Conventions in three fourths thereof, as the one or the other Mode of Ratification may be proposed by the Congress; Provided that no Amendment which may be made prior to the Year One thousand eight hundred and eight shall in any Manner affect the first and fourth Clauses in the Ninth Section of the first Article; and that no State, without its Consent, shall be deprived of its equal Suffrage in the Senate.

Article VI

All Debts contracted and Engagements entered into, before the Adoption of this Constitution, shall be as valid against the United States under this Constitution, as under the Confederation.

This Constitution, and the Laws of the United States which shall be made in Pursuance thereof; and all Treaties made, or which shall be made, under the Authority of the United States, shall be the supreme Law of the Land; and the Judges in every State shall be bound thereby, any Thing in the Constitution or Laws of any State to the Contrary not with-standing.

The Senators and Representatives before mentioned, and the Members of the several State Legislatures, and all executive and judicial Officers, both of the United States and of the several States, shall be bound by Oath or Affirmation, to support this Constitution; but no religious Test shall ever be required as a Qualification to any Office or public Trust under the United States.

Article VII

The Ratification of the Conventions of nine States shall be sufficient for the Establishment of this Constitution between the States so ratifying the Same.

Done in Convention by the Unanimous Consent of the States present the Seventeenth Day of September in the Year of our Lord one thousand seven hundred and Eighty seven and of the Independence of the United States of America the Twelfth

IN WITNESS whereof We have hereunto subscribed our Names,

George Washington–President and deputy from Virginia
New Hampshire: John Langdon, Nicholas Gilman
Massachusetts: Nathaniel Gorham, Rufus King
Connecticut: William Samuel Johnson, Roger Sherman
New York: Alexander Hamilton
New Jersey: William Livingston, David Brearly, William Paterson,

Jonathan Dayton
Pennsylvania: Benjamin Franklin, Thomas Mifflin, Robert Morris, George Clymer, Thomas FitzSimons, Jared Ingersoll, James Wilson, Gouverneur Morris
Delaware: George Read, Gunning Bedford, Jr., John Dickinson, Richard Bassett, Jacob Broom
Maryland: James McHenry, Daniel of Saint Thomas Jenifer, Daniel Carroll
Virginia: John Blair, James Madison, Jr.
North Carolina: William Blount, Richard Dobbs Spaight, Hugh Williamson
South Carolina: John Rutledge, Charles Cotesworth Pinckney, Charles Pinckney, Pierce Butler
Georgia: William Few, Abraham Baldwin

Amendments To
The U.S. Constitution

Amendment 1 - Freedom of Religion, Press, Expression. Congress shall make no law respecting an establishment of religion, or prohibiting the free exercise thereof; or abridging the freedom of speech, or of the press; or the right of the people peaceably to assemble, and to petition the Government for a redress of grievances.

Amendment 2 - Right to Bear Arms. A well-regulated Militia, being necessary to the security of a free State, the right of the people to keep and bear Arms, shall not be infringed.

Amendment 3 - Quartering of Soldiers. No Soldier shall, in time of peace be quartered in any house, without the consent of the Owner, nor in time of war, but in a manner to be prescribed by law.

Amendment 4 - Search and Seizure. The right of the people to be secure in their persons, houses, papers, and effects, against unreasonable searches and seizures, shall not be violated, and no Warrants shall issue, but upon probable cause, supported by Oath or affirmation, and particularly describing the place to be searched, and the persons or things to be seized.

Amendment 5 - Trial and Punishment, Compensation for Takings. No person shall be held to answer for a capital, or otherwise infamous crime, unless on a presentment or indictment of a Grand Jury, except in cases arising in the land or naval forces, or in the Militia, when in actual service in time of War or public danger; nor shall any person be subject for the same offense to be twice put in jeopardy of life or limb; nor shall be compelled in any criminal case to be a witness against himself, nor be deprived of life, liberty, or property, without due process of law; nor shall private property be taken for public use, without just compensation.

Amendment 6 - Right to Speedy Trial, Confrontation of Witnesses. In all criminal prosecutions, the accused shall enjoy the right to a speedy and public trial, by an impartial jury of the State and district wherein the crime shall have been committed, which district shall have been previously ascertained by law, and to be informed of the nature and cause of the accusation; to be confronted with the witnesses against him; to have compulsory process for obtaining witnesses in his favor, and to have the Assistance of Counsel for his defence.

Amendment 7 - Trial by Jury in Civil Cases. In Suits at common law, where the value in controversy shall exceed twenty dollars, the right of trial by jury shall be preserved, and no fact tried by a jury, shall be otherwise re-examined in any Court of the United States, than according to the rules of the common law.

Amendment 8 - Cruel and Unusual Punishment. Excessive bail shall not be required, nor excessive fines imposed, nor cruel and unusual punishments inflicted.

Amendment 9 - Construction of Constitution. The enumeration in the Constitution, of certain rights, shall not be construed to deny or disparage others retained by the people.

Amendment 10 - Powers of the States and People. The powers not delegated to the United States by the Constitution, nor prohibited by it to the States, are reserved to the States respectively, or to the people.

THIS IS THE END OF THE ORIGINAL AMENDMENTS TO THE CONSTITUTION THAT WERE REQUIRED BY THE

STATES IN EXCHANGE FOR ITS PASSAGE, AND MUST BE CONSIDERED A PART OF THE DOCUMENT ITSELF.

Subsequent Amendments:

Amendment 11 - Judicial Limits. The Judicial power of the United States shall not be construed to extend to any suit in law or equity, commenced or prosecuted against one of the United States by Citizens of another State, or by Citizens or Subjects of any Foreign State.

Amendment 12 - Choosing the President, Vice-President. The Electors shall meet in their respective states, and vote by ballot for President and Vice-President, one of whom, at least, shall not be an inhabitant of the same state with themselves; they shall name in their ballots the person voted for as President, and in distinct ballots the person voted for as Vice-President, and they shall make distinct lists of all persons voted for as President, and of all persons voted for as Vice-President and of the number of votes for each, which lists they shall sign and certify, and transmit sealed to the seat of the government of the United States, directed to the President of the Senate;

The President of the Senate shall, in the presence of the Senate and House of Representatives, open all the certificates and the votes shall then be counted;

The person having the greatest Number of votes for President, shall be the President, if such number be a majority of the whole number of Electors appointed; and if no person have such majority, then from the persons having the highest numbers not exceeding three on the list of those voted for as President, the House of Representatives shall choose immediately, by ballot, the President. But in choosing the President, the votes shall be taken by states, the representation from each state having one vote; a quorum for this purpose shall consist of a member or members from two-thirds of the states, and a majority of all the states shall be necessary to a choice. And if the House of Representatives shall not choose a President whenever the right of choice shall devolve upon them, before the fourth day of March next following, then the Vice-President shall act as President, as in the case of the death or other constitutional disability of the President.

The person having the greatest number of votes as Vice-President, shall be the Vice-President, if such number be a majority of the whole number of Electors appointed, and if no person have a majority, then from the two highest numbers on the list, the Senate shall choose the Vice-President a quorum for the purpose shall consist of two-thirds of the whole number of Senators, and a majority of the whole number shall be necessary to a choice. But no person constitutionally ineligible to the office of President shall be eligible to that of Vice-President of the United States.

Amendment 13 - Slavery Abolished.

1. Neither slavery nor involuntary servitude, except as a punishment for crime whereof the party shall have been duly convicted, shall exist with in the United States, or any place subject to their jurisdiction.

2. Congress shall have power to enforce this article by appropriate legislation.

Amendment 14 - Citizenship Rights.

1. All persons born or naturalized in the United States, and subject to the jurisdiction thereof, are citizens of the United States and of the State wherein they reside. No State shall make or enforce any law which shall abridge the privileges or immunities of citizens of the United States; nor shall any State deprive any person of life, liberty, or property, without due process of law; nor deny to any person within its jurisdiction the equal protection of the laws.

2. Representatives shall be apportioned among the several States according to their respective numbers, counting the whole number of persons in each State, excluding Indians not taxed. But when the right to vote at any election for the choice of electors for President and Vice-President of the United States, Representatives in Congress, the Executive and Judicial officers of a State, or the members of the Legislature thereof, is denied to any of the male inhabitants of such State, being twenty-one years of age, and citizens of the United States, or in any way abridged, except for participation in rebellion, or other crime, the basis of representation therein shall be reduced in the proportion which the number of such male citizens shall bear to the whole number of male citizens twenty-one years of age in such State.

3. No person shall be a Senator or Representative in Congress, or elector of President and Vice-President, or hold any office, civil or military, under the United States, or under any State, who, having previously taken an oath, as a member of Congress, or as an officer of the United States, or as a member of any State legislature, or as an executive or judicial officer of any State, to support the Constitution of the United States, shall have engaged in insurrection or rebellion against the same, or given aid or comfort to the enemies thereof. But Congress may by a vote of two-thirds of each House, remove such disability.

4. The validity of the public debt of the United States, authorized by law, including debts incurred for payment of pensions and bounties for services in suppressing insurrection or rebellion, shall not be questioned. But neither the United States nor any State shall assume or pay any debt or obligation incurred in aid of insurrection or rebellion against the United States, or any claim for the loss or emancipation of any slave; but all such debts, obligations and claims shall be held illegal and void.

5. The Congress shall have power to enforce, by appropriate legislation, the provisions of this article.

Amendment 15 - Race No Bar to Vote.

1. The right of citizens of the United States to vote shall not be denied or abridged by the United States or by any State on account of race, color, or previous condition of servitude.

2. The Congress shall have power to enforce this article by appropriate legislation.

Amendment 16 - Status of Income Tax Clarified. The Congress shall have power to lay and collect taxes on incomes, from whatever source derived, without apportionment among the several States, and without regard to any census or enumeration.

Amendment 17 - Senators Elected by Popular Vote. The Senate of the United States shall be composed of two Senators from each State, elected by the people thereof, for six years; and each

Senator shall have one vote. The electors in each State shall have the qualifications requisite for electors of the most numerous branch of the State legislatures.

When vacancies happen in the representation of any State in the Senate, the executive authority of such State shall issue writs of election to fill such vacancies: Provided, That the legislature of any State may empower the executive thereof to make temporary appointments until the people fill the vacancies by election as the legislature may direct.

This amendment shall not be so construed as to affect the election or term of any Senator chosen before it becomes valid as part of the Constitution.

Amendment 18 - Liquor Abolished.

1. After one year from the ratification of this article the manufacture, sale, or transportation of intoxicating liquors within, the importation thereof into, or the exportation thereof from the United States and all territory subject to the jurisdiction thereof for beverage purposes is hereby prohibited.

2. The Congress and the several States shall have concurrent power to enforce this article by appropriate legislation.

3. This article shall be inoperative unless it shall have been ratified as an amendment to the Constitution by the legislatures of the several States, as provided in the Constitution, within seven years from the date of the submission hereof to the States by the Congress.

Amendment 19 - Women's Suffrage. The right of citizens of the United States to vote shall not be denied or abridged by the United States or by any State on account of sex.

Congress shall have power to enforce this article by appropriate legislation.

Amendment 20 - Presidential, Congressional Terms.

1. The terms of the President and Vice President shall end at noon on the 20th day of January, and the terms of Senators and Representatives at noon on the 3d day of January, of the years in which such terms would have ended if this article had not been ratified; and the terms of their successors shall then begin.

2. The Congress shall assemble at least once in every year, and such meeting shall begin at noon on the 3d day of January, unless they shall by law appoint a different day.

3. If, at the time fixed for the beginning of the term of the President, the President elect shall have died, the Vice President elect shall become President. If a President shall not have been chosen before the time fixed for the beginning of his term, or if the President elect shall have failed to qualify, then the Vice President elect shall act as President until a President shall have qualified; and the Congress may by law provide for the case wherein neither a President elect nor a Vice President elect shall have qualified, declaring who shall then act as President, or the manner

in which one who is to act shall be selected, and such person shall act accordingly until a President or Vice President shall have qualified.

4. The Congress may by law provide for the case of the death of any of the persons from whom the House of Representatives may choose a President whenever the right of choice shall have devolved upon them, and for the case of the death of any of the persons from whom the Senate may choose a Vice President whenever the right of choice shall have devolved upon them.

5. Sections 1 and 2 shall take effect on the 15th day of October following the ratification of this article.

6. This article shall be inoperative unless it shall have been ratified as an amendment to the Constitution by the legislatures of three-fourths of the several States within seven years from the date of its submission.

Amendment 21 - Amendment 18 Repealed.

1. The eighteenth article of amendment to the Constitution of the United States is hereby repealed.

2. The transportation or importation into any State, Territory, or possession of the United States for delivery or use therein of intoxicating liquors, in violation of the laws thereof, is hereby prohibited.

3. The article shall be inoperative unless it shall have been ratified as an amendment to the Constitution by conventions in the several States, as provided in the Constitution, within seven years from the date of the submission hereof to the States by the Congress.

Amendment 22 - Presidential Term Limits.

1. No person shall be elected to the office of the President more than twice, and no person who has held the office of President, or acted as President, for more than two years of a term to which some other person was elected President shall be elected to the office of the President

more than once. But this Article shall not apply to any person holding the office of President, when this Article was proposed by the Congress, and shall not prevent any person who may be holding the office of President, or acting as President, during the term within which this Article becomes operative from holding the office of President or acting as President during the remainder of such term.

2. This article shall be inoperative unless it shall have been ratified as an amendment to the Constitution by the legislatures of three-fourths of the several States within seven years from the date of its submission to the States by the Congress.

Amendment 23 - Presidential Vote for District of Columbia.

1. The District constituting the seat of Government of the United States shall appoint in such manner as the Congress may direct: A number of electors of President and Vice President equal to the whole number of Senators and Representatives in Congress to which the District would be entitled if it were a State, but in no event more than the least populous State; they shall be in addition to those appointed by the States, but they shall be considered, for the purposes of the election of President and Vice President, to be electors appointed by a State; and they shall meet in the District and perform such duties as provided by the twelfth article of amendment.

2. The Congress shall have power to enforce this article by appropriate legislation.

Amendment 24 - Poll Tax Barred.

1. The right of citizens of the United States to vote in any primary or other election for President or Vice President, for electors for President or Vice President, or for Senator or Representative in Congress, shall not be denied or abridged by the United States or any State by reason of failure to pay any poll tax or other tax.

2. The Congress shall have power to enforce this article by appropriate legislation.

Amendment 25 - Presidential Disability and Succession.

1. In case of the removal of the President from office or of his death or resignation, the Vice President shall become President.

2. Whenever there is a vacancy in the office of the Vice President, the President shall nominate a Vice President who shall take office upon confirmation by a majority vote of both Houses of Congress.

3. Whenever the President transmits to the President pro tempore of the Senate and the Speaker of the House of Representatives his written declaration that he is unable to discharge the powers and duties of his office, and until he transmits to them a written declaration to the contrary, such powers and duties shall be discharged by the Vice President as Acting President.

4. Whenever the Vice President and a majority of either the principal officers of the executive departments or of such other body as Congress may by law provide, transmit to the President pro tempore of the Senate and the Speaker of the House of Representatives their written declaration that the President is unable to discharge the powers and duties of his office, the Vice President shall immediately assume the powers and duties of the office as Acting President.

Thereafter, when the President transmits to the President pro tempore of the Senate and the Speaker of the House of Representatives his written declaration that no inability exists, he shall resume the powers and duties of his office unless the Vice President and a majority of either the principal officers of the executive department or of such other body as Congress may by law provide, transmit within four days to the President pro tempore of the Senate and the Speaker of the House of Representatives their written declaration that the President is unable to discharge the powers and duties of his office. Thereupon Congress shall decide the issue, assembling within forty eight hours for that purpose if not in session. If the Congress, within twenty one days after receipt of the latter written declaration, or, if Congress is not in session, within twenty one days after Congress is required to assemble, determines by two thirds vote of both Houses that the President is unable to discharge the powers and duties of his office, the Vice President shall continue to discharge the same as Acting President; otherwise, the President shall resume the powers and duties of his office.

Amendment 26 - Voting Age Set to 18 Years.

1. The right of citizens of the United States, who are eighteen years of age or older, to vote shall not be denied or abridged by the United States or by any State on account of age.

2. The Congress shall have power to enforce this article by appropriate legislation.

Amendment 27 - Limiting Changes to Congressional Pay. No law, varying the compensation for the services of the Senators and Representatives, shall take effect, until an election of Representatives shall have intervened.

APPENDIX B
AMENDMENT 14 AS APPLIED TO CORPORATIONS

[Equal Protection]

SECTION 1- "All persons born or naturalized in the United States, and subject to the jurisdiction thereof, are citizens of the United States where they reside. No State shall make or enforce any law which shall abridge the privileges or immunities citizens of the United States, nor shall any State deprive any person of life, liberty, property, without due process of law; nor deny to any person within its jurisdiction the equal protection of the laws."

b. Business Corporations

1602. Generally

Corporation is as much entitled to equal protection of laws as individual. Frost v Corporation Com. of Oklahoma (1929) 278 US 515, 73 L Ed 483, 49 , S Ct 235; Louis K. Uggett Co. v Lee (1933) 288 US 517, 77 L Ed 929, 53 S Ct 481, 85 ALR 699.

Differences in organization and purpose between co-operatives and other business organizations justify different treatment of them for regulatory purposes. United States v Rock Royal Co-operative, Inc. (1939)

307 US 533, 83 L Ed 1446, 59 S Ct 993, reh den (1939) 308 US 631, 84 L Ed 526, 60 S Ct 66, 60 S Ct 67.

1603. Corporation as person

Corporation is person within meaning of Fourteenth Amendment which forbids state to deny to any person within its jurisdiction equal protection of laws. Santa Clara County v Southern P. R. Co. (1886) 118 US 394, 30 L Ed 118, 6 S Ct 1132; Pembina Consol. Silver Mining & Milling Co. v Pennsylvania (1888) 125 US 181, 31 L Ed 650, 8 S, Ct 737; Missouri P. R. Co. v Mackey (1888) 127 US 205. 32 L Ed 107, 8 S Q 1161; Minneapolis & S. L. R. Co. v Herrick (1888) 127 US 210, 32 L Ed 109, 8 S Q 1176; Minneapolis & S. L. R. Co. v Beckwith (1889) 129 US 26, 32 L Ed 585, 9 S d 207; Charlotte, C. & A. R. Co. v Gibbes (1892) 142 US 386, 35 L Ed 1051, 12 S Ct 255; Gulf, C. & S. F. R. Co. v Ellis (1897) 165 US 150, 41 L Ed 666, 17 S Ct 255; Southern R. Co. v Greene (1910) 216 US 400, 54 L Ed 536, 30 S Q 287.

Corporations are persons within meaning of Fourteenth Amendment of Constitution of United States, and can invoke benefits of provisions of Constitution and laws which guarantee to persons enjoyment of property, or afford to them means for its protection, or prohibit legislation injuriously affecting it Missouri P. R. Co. v Mackey (1888) 127 US 205, 32 L Ed 107, 8 S Ct 1161; Minneapolis & S. L, R. Co. v Henick (1888) 127 US 210, 32 L Ed 109, 8 S Ct 1176.

Corporation is person within meaning of both due process and equal protection clauses of Fourteenth Amendment to Federal Constitution. Covington & Lexington Turnpike Road Co. v Sanford (1896) 164 US 578, 41 L Ed 560, 17 S Cl 198; Kentucky Finance Corp. v Paramount Auto Exchange Corp. (1923) 262 US 544, 67 L Ed 1112, 43 S Ct 636; Grosjean v American Press Co. (1936) 297 US 233, 80 L Ed 660. 56 S Q 444, 1 Media L R 2685.

Corporations may not arbitrarily be selected in order to be subjected to burden to which individuals would as appropriately be subject. Mallinckrodt Chemical Works v Missouri (1913) 238 US 41, 59 LEd 1192, 35 SCI 671.

Inherent difference between corporations and natural persons is sufficient to sustain classification making restrictions upon right of nonresidents to do business in state applicable to corporations alone. Crescent Cotton Oil Co, v Mississippi (1921) 257 US 129, 66 L Ed 166,42 S Ct 42.

1604. Corporation as citizen

Corporation has same rights to protection of laws as natural citizen. Home Ins. Co. v Morse (1874) 87 US 445, 20 Wall 445, 22 L Ed 365 (superseded by statute on other grounds as stated in Sverdrup Corp. v WHC Constructors, Inc. (1993, CA4 SC) 989 F2d 148).

1605. Monopolies end restraint of trade

Possible invalidity as to individuals of provisions of Ark. act, Jan. 23, 1905, § 1, penalizing doing of business within state by members of trust or combination to control prices, does not render such provisions invalid as to corporations, as denying equal protection of laws. Hammond Packing Co. v Arkansas (1909) 212 US 322, 53 L Ed 530, 29 S Ct 370. Insurance company connected with tariff association which fixes rates is not denied equal protection...

Appendix C
Amendment 16

[Income Tax]

"The Congress shall have power to lay and collect taxes on incomes, from whatever source derived, without apportionment among the several States, and without regard to any census or enumeration."

History; Ancillary Laws And Directives

EXPLANATORY notes:

The Sixteenth Amendment to the Constitution of the United States was proposed to the legislatures of the several states by the Sixty-first Congress on July 12, 1909, and was declared, in a proclamation of the Secretary of State, dated February 25, 1913, to have been ratified by the legislatures of the following states: Alabama, August 10, 1909; Arizona, April 6, 1912; Arkansas, April 22, 1911; California, January 31, 1911; Colorado, February 15, 1911; Delaware, February 3, 1913; Georgia, August 3, 1910; Idaho, January 20, 1911; Illinois, March 1, 1910; Indiana, January 30, 1911; Iowa, February 24, 1911; Kansas, February 18, 1911; Kentucky, February 8, 1910; Louisiana, June 28, 1912; Maine, March 31, 1911; Maryland, April

8, 1910; Michigan; February 23, 1911; Minnesota, June, It, 1912; Mississippi, March 7, 1910; Missouri, March 16, 1911; Montana, January 30, 1911; Nebraska, February 9, 1911; Nevada, January 31, 1911; New Mexico, February 3, 1913; New York, July 12, 1911; North Carolina, February 11, 1911; North Dakota, February 17, 1911; Ohio, January 19, 1911; Oklahoma, March 10, 1910; Oregon, January 23, 1911; South Carolina, February 19, 1910; South Dakota, February 3, 1911; Tennessee, April-7, 1911; Texas, August 16, 1910; Washington, January 26, 1911; West Virginia, January 31, 1913; "Wisconsin, May 26, 1911; and Wyoming, February 3, 1913.

Ratification was completed on February 3, 1913. The amendment was subsequently ratified by New Jersey, February 5, 1913; Massachusetts, March 14, 1913; and New Hampshire, March 7, 1913.

The amendment was rejected, and not subsequently ratified, by Connecticut, Rhode Island, and Utah.

Research Guide

Law Review Articles:

Kornhauser. The constitutional meaning of income and the income taxation of gifts. 25 Conn L Rev 1, Fall 1992.

Choper. The Scope of National Power Vis-a-Vis the States: The Dispensability of Judicial Review. 86 Yale L J 1552.

INTERPRETIVE NOTES AND DECISIONS

1. Generally

2. Validity of Amendment

3. Relation to other Constitutional provisions

4. General scope of Congressional authority

5. Effect of state laws

6. What is "income"

7. Sales proceeds

8. Dividends

9. Insurance

10. Gifts

11. Government payments to railroads

12. Other

13. Who is subject to tax

14. State agencies and employees

15. Citizens residing outside country

1. Generally

Sixteenth Amendment does not extend taxing power to new or excepted subjects, but merely removes all occasion for apportionment among states of taxes laid on income from whatever source. William E. Peck & Co. v Lowe (1918) 247 US 165, 62 L Ed 1049, 38 S. Ct 432, 1 USTC 16, 3 AFTR 2971; Bowers v Kerbailgh-Empire Co. (1926) 271 US 170, 70 L Ed 886, 46 S Ct 449, 1 USTC § 174, 5 AFTR 6014; Sprouse v Commissioner (1941, CA9) 122 F2d 973,41-2 USTC § 9703,28 AFTR I, 143 ALR 226, affd (1943) 318 US 604, 87 L Ed 1029, 63 S Ct 791, 43- 1 USTC § 9363, 30 AFTR 1087, 144 ALR 1335.

2. Validity of Amendment

Sixteenth Amendment was constitutionally adopted. Brushaber v Union P. R, Co. (1916) 240 US 1, 60 L.Ed 493, 36 S Ct 236, 1 USTC 4, 3 AFTR 2926.

In prosecution under 26 USCS §§ 7201 and 7203 for "willfully" attempting to evade federal income taxes and "willfully" failing to file federal income tax returns, defendant's views about validity of tax statutes, and Sixteenth Amendment are irrelevant to issue of willfulness and need not be heard by jury. Cheek v United States (1991) 498 US 192, 112 L Ed 2d 617, 111 S Ct 604, 91 CDOS 305, 91 Daily Journal DAR 371, 91-1 USTC§ 50012, 67 AFTR 2d 344, on remand, remanded (1991, CA7 HI) 931 F2d 1206, 91-1 USTC § 50232, 67 AFTR 2d 965.

Action to recover sura paid on declaration of estimated income tax, was without merit, far-fetched, and frivolous, where based on allegations that Sixteenth Amendment was illegal because it placed taxpayer in position of involuntary servitude and that subsequent federal tax legislation had given rise to mass of ambiguous, contradictory, inequitable, and unjust rules, regulations, and methods of procedure so as to jeopardize taxpayer's rights as citizen by compelling him to assume unreasonable obligations and burdens to make just accounting of his income and pay tax thereon. Forth v Brodrick (1954, CA10 Kan) 214 F2d 925, 54-2 USTC § 9552, 46 AFTR 515.

Sixteenth Amendment is effective legal document, even though only four states ratified its language exactly as Congress approved it—other versions containing errors of diction, capitalization, punctuation, and spelling—since, inter alia, in 1913 the Secretary of State declared it adopted, and Supreme Court follows "enrolled bill rule" providing that if legislative document is authenticated in regular form by appropriate officials, that document is treated as adopted. United States v Thomas (1986, CAT 111) 788 F2d 1250, 86-1 USTC 1 9354, 57 AFTR 2d 1215, cert den (1986) 479 US 853, 93 L Ed 2d 121, 107 S Ct 187.

That Sixteenth Amendment had been in existence for 73 years and had been applied by the Supreme Court in countless cases, was very persuasive on question of its validity; taxpayer failed to make exceptionally strong showing of unconstitutional ratification where he contended, inter alia, that of 36 states tendering Sixteenth Amendment ratifying resolutions to State Department, 11 states had adopted versions with different wording, 22 states had altered its punctuation, and one state bad actually rejected, it United States v Foster (1986, CA7 HI) 789 F2d 457, 86-1 USTC § 9327, 57,AFTR 2d 1150, cert den (1986) 479 US 883, 93 LEd 2d 249, 107 S Ct 273.

Sixteenth Amendment was properly ratified. United States v Ferguson (1986, CA7 Ind) 793 F2d 828,86-1 USTC § 9475,58 AFTR 2d 5179, cert den (1986) 479 US 933, 93 L Ed 2d 358, 107 S Ct 406.

Advancing argument, totally unfounded, that Sixteenth Amendment was not ratified by requisite number of states, will result in imposition of sanctions against taxpayer. Cook v Spillman (1986, CA9 Cal) 806 F2d 948, 87-1 USTC § 9121, 59 AFTR 2d 665.

Arguments that Sixteenth Amendment was never ratified by required number of states because of errors in ratification process and that Secretary of State committed fraud by certifying adoption of Amendment are frivolous, in that Secretary of State is bound by State's notification of ratification, and respect for coordinate branches of government prevents judicial review of Secretary of State's official certification of ratification. Pollard v Commissioner, 1RS (1987, CA11) 816 F2d 603,87-1 USTC § 9314, 59 AFTR 2d 1074.

Validity of ratification of Sixteenth Amendment is now beyond review, and petitioner's contention that be is uniquely qualified, as author of historical analysis of amendment, to make "exceptionally strong showing" required for evidentiary hearing will be rejected. United States v Benson (1991, CA7 III) 941 F2d 598, 91-2 USTC § 50437, 34 Fed Rules Evid

Serv 579, 68 AFTR 2d 5469, reh, en banc, den (1992, CA7) 1992 US App LEXIS 425 and amd (1992, CA7 HI) 957 F2d 301.

Frivolous challenges to 16th Amendment and income tax legislation and regulations will result in imposition of full range of sanctions provided by Rule 38 of Federal Rules of Appellate Procedure. Sochia v Commissioner (1994, CA5 Tex) 23 F3d 941, 94-2 USTC § 50338, 29 FR

Serv 3d 742, 74...